Minimal Ethics for the Anthropocene

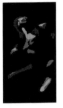

Critical Climate Change

SERIES EDITORS: TOM COHEN AND CLAIRE COLEBROOK

The era of climate change involves the mutation of systems beyond 20th century anthropomorphic models and has stood, until recently, outside representation or address. Understood in a broad and critical sense, climate change concerns material agencies that impact on biomass and energy, erased borders and microbial invention, geological and nanographic time, and extinction events. The possibility of extinction has always been a latent figure in textual production and archives; but the current sense of depletion, decay, mutation and exhaustion calls for new modes of address, new styles of publishing and authoring, and new formats and speeds of distribution. As the pressures and re-alignments of this re-arrangement occur, so must the critical languages and conceptual templates, political premises and definitions of 'life.' There is a particular need to publish in timely fashion experimental monographs that redefine the boundaries of disciplinary fields, rhetorical invasions, the interface of conceptual and scientific languages, and geomorphic and geopolitical interventions. Critical Climate Change is oriented, in this general manner, toward the epistemo-political mutations that correspond to the temporalities of terrestrial mutation.

Minimal Ethics for the Anthropocene

Joanna Zylinska

( )

OPEN HUMANITIES PRESS

An imprint of Michigan Publishing
University of Michigan Library, Ann Arbor

2014

First edition published by OPEN HUMANITIES PRESS 2014

Freely available online at http://dx.doi.org/10.3998/ohp.12917741.0001.001

ISBN-13 978-1-60785-329-9

OPEN HUMANITIES PRESS is an international, scholar-led open access publishing collective whose mission is to make leading works of contemporary critical thought freely available worldwide. Books published under the OPEN HUMANITIES PRESS imprint at Michigan Publishing are produced through a unique partnership between OHP's editorial board and the University of Michigan Library, which provides a library-based managing and production support infrastructure to facilitate scholars to publish leading research in book form.

MICHIGAN
PUBLISHING
www.publishing.umich.edu

O
OPEN HUMANITIES PRESS
www.openhumanitiespress.org

Contents

Fig. 1: Joanna Zylinska, *Topia daedala* 1, 2014

Acknowledgments

This book was inspired by Annie Sprinkle and Beth Stephens' wonderfully provocative wedding to Lake Kallavesi at the ANTI Contemporary Art Festival in Kuopio, Finland, in September 2012. I am grateful to Annie and Beth, and to Luke Dixon, for allowing me to develop further my ideas on ethics and the Anthropocene at their 2013 Ecosex Symposium at Colchester Art Centre in England. Many other people have generously provided a space—both mental and physical—for me to experiment with this project, in different guises. I am particularly grateful to my antipodean friends (Nina Sellars, Stelarc, Oron Catts and Ionat Zurr of SymbioticA) as well as the innumerable generous interlocutors from Mexico (Ana María Martínez de la Escalera from UNAM; Alberto López Cuenca and Gabriela Méndez Cota from UDLAP; the Transitio MX_05 festival team and its guests), Kate O'Riordan and Btihaj Ajana. I owe a big thank-you to many of my Goldsmiths colleagues and students, for keeping both the question of critical thinking and the question of politics permanently alive and open. Last but not least, I am grateful to Sarah Kember, Sigi Jöttkandt, David Ottina and Gary Hall.

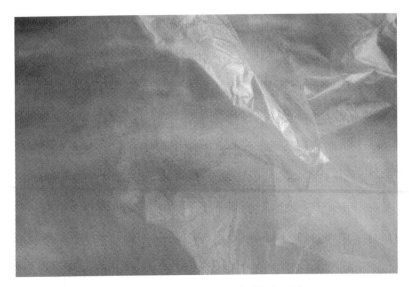

Fig. 2: Joanna Zylinska, *Topia daedala* 2, 2014

Chapter 1

Grounding

Life typically becomes an object of reflection when it is seen to be under threat. In particular, we humans have a tendency to engage in thinking about life (instead of just continuing to live it) when we are made to confront the prospect of death: be it the death of individuals due to illness, accident or old age; the death of whole ethnic or national groups in wars and other forms of armed conflict; but also of whole populations, be it human or nonhuman ones. Even though this book is first and foremost about life—comprehended as both a biological and social phenomenon—it is the narrative about the impending death of the human population, i.e., about the extinction of the human species, that provides a context for its argument. In contemporary popular science and mainstream media the problem of extinction is usually presented as something both inevitable and impending. To cite the British scientist Stephen Emmott, head of Microsoft's Computational Science research and co-author of the book *Ten Billion*,[1] the current situation in which the human species finds itself can be most adequately described with the phrase "we are

fucked". The reasons for this supposed state of events
are as follows:

> Earth is home to millions of species. Just
> one dominates it. Us. Our cleverness, our
> inventiveness and our activities have mod-
> ified almost every part of our planet. In
> fact, we are having a profound impact on
> it. Indeed, our cleverness, our inventive-
> ness and our activities are now the drivers
> of every global problem we face. And every
> one of these problems is accelerating as we
> continue to grow towards a global popula-
> tion of ten billion. In fact, I believe we can
> rightly call the situation we're in right now
> an emergency—an unprecedented plan-
> etary emergency. (non-pag.)

This unique situation, or rather geo-historical period,
in which humans are said to have become the biggest
threat to life on earth, has recently gained the moniker
"Anthropocene". Emmott's practical solution to this
situation is rather blunt: given that any possible technological or behavioral solutions to the current state
of events, even if theoretically possible, are unlikely
to work, the advice he would give his son would
be to "buy a gun". This is of course a powerful story,
the goal of which is to shock and awe us into action.
Without shooting our gun-wielding messenger, it is
worth pointing out that there seems to be something
both defeatist and narcissistic about jeremiads of this
kind and those that tell them. Also, we humans have
actually produced narratives about different forms of

apocalypse ever since we developed the ability to tell stories and record them.

Rather than add to this catalogue, my aim in this book is to tell a different story about the world and our human positioning in and with it, while taking seriously what science has to say about life and death. I am mindful of philosopher John Gray's admonition in his review of Emmott's book that "The planet does not care about the stories that humans tell themselves; it responds to what humans do, and is changing irreversibly as a result" (6). Gray is no doubt correct in his skepticism. Yet it should be noted that we humans *do* care about the stories we tell ourselves. More importantly, stories have a performative nature: they can enact and not just describe things—even if there are of course limits to what they are capable of enacting. This book is one such story about life and death at both macro and micro scales, shaped into a set of philosophical propositions for non-philosophers. More specifically, its aim is to outline a viable position on ethics as a way of living a good life when life itself is declared to be under a unique threat. In other words, it is a story about how we can live a good life at this precarious geo-historical moment—and about what constitutes such goodness.

The injunction to outline some kind of "teaching of the good life" (Adorno 15) when life itself is said to be under threat comes to me partly from Theodor Adorno's *Minima Moralia*, a 1944 slim volume by the Frankfurt philosopher written as a gift to his friend and collaborator Max Horkheimer, and subtitled

Reflections on a Damaged Life. On one level, Adorno's diagnosis seems to be similar in tenor to Emmott's:

> Life has changed into a timeless succession of shocks, interspaced with empty, paralysed intervals. But nothing, perhaps, is more ominous for the future than the fact that, quite literally, these things will soon be past thinking on, for each trauma of the returning combatants, each shock not inwardly absorbed, is a ferment of future destruction. Karl Kraus was right to call his play *The Last Days of Mankind*. What is being enacted now ought to bear the title: "After Doomsday". (54)

Yet the context of Adorno's reflections, themselves presented in a series of fragments and what we might term "shards of thought", is very unique: they spring from what he perceives as life's catastrophic and irreparable destruction in the Holocaust. Bemoaning the fact that others are already envisaging the possibility of "rebuilding culture" as if the murder of millions of Jews had been just an unpleasant interlude, he sees modern life as reduced "to the sphere of the private and then merely consumption", a state of events that leads to alienation and the withdrawal of vitality from life itself. Citing the Austrian writer Ferdinand Kürnberger, Adorno laments that "Life does not live". But Adorno does not stop because of that: instead, he goes on looking for life's traces buried in language, and for the possibility of continuing with critical thought and writing, with a determination to teach us about "the good life", even if on a very small scale.

My own project on minimal ethics draws inspiration from Adorno's persistence in *Minima Moralia* to keep philosophizing as if against all odds, to look for signs of life in the middle of an apocalypse, even if my own context and the existential threats that shape it are very different from his. The ambition and orientation of my ethical propositions also differ from Adorno's: even though I embrace the critical spirit of his work, I turn to various philosophies of life as well as feminist thought in order to outline a more affirmative framework for the times when life is said to find itself under threat on a planetary scale. My aim here is for us to consider to what extent we can make life go on and also how we ourselves can continue to live it well, while interrogating what it means "to live life well", and whether such a consensus can actually be reached.

It needs to be signaled right from the start that the very "we" of the argument that will ensue is also already posited as a problem, referring as it does to what philosophy and common sense have designated as "humans" but also opening onto a complex and dynamic network of relations in which "we humans" are produced as humans and in which we remain entangled with nonhuman entities and processes. The seeds of this book were originally planted during the preparations for a wedding of ecosex artists Beth Stephens and Annie Sprinkle, who married Lake Kallavesi—which is part of the Iso-Kalla lake system in Northern Savonia—at the ANTI Contemporary

Art Festival in Kuopio, Finland, on September 30, 2012. (I wrote a short piece on minimal ethics as a wedding gift for them.) This human-nonhuman wedding between more than two parties was not Stephens and Sprinkle's first: in previous ceremonies they had married the Earth, the Sea, the Snow and the Rocks, thus playfully taking on and enacting the naturocultural kinship in which *love is not enough*. Stephens and Sprinkle's performance serves for me as an entry point into a different mode of philosophizing, one that borrows from artistic sensibilities and that produces ideas with things and events rather than *just* with words. This mode of philosophical production is necessarily fragmented: it gives up on any desire to forge systems, ontologies or worlds and makes itself content with minor, even if abundant, interventions into material and conceptual unfoldings. A minimal ethics outlined throughout this book is one such possible intervention.

The mode of working employed in this book mobilizes what could be termed "a post-masculinist rationality", a more speculative, less directional mode of thinking and writing. This notion develops from Darin Barney's concept of post-masculinist courage. For Barney, "courage that is *post-masculinist* is not necessarily therefore *feminine* (or even really *post-masculine*—though it is very likely to be feminist)" (nonpag.). Barney's call is in turn inspired by political theorist Wendy Brown, who has outlined a vision for "a post-masculinist politics" in which freedom is reconciled with love and recognition. Such politics requires "much courage and willingness to risk" (Brown 202).

Barney suggests this sort of courage needs to be distinguished from "the sort of bravado whereby men seek to exert control over everything around them by the force of instrumental rationality" (non-pag.). Post-masculinist courage involves for him "the courage to face the uncertainty of that which we cannot control; [...] the courage to be let go into action that begins something truly new and unpredictable" (non-pag.). A post-masculinist rationality is by no means non- or anti-rationalist; it just calls for a different modulation of rationality, one that remains more attuned to its own modes of production. It is always already embodied and immersed, responding to the call of matter and to its various materializations—materializations such as humans, animals, plants, inanimate objects, as well as the relations between them. Such post-masculinist rationality remains suspicious towards any current attempts to (re)turn to ontology, in both its idealist and materialist guises, as a predominant mode of philosophizing. It sees any such attempts for what they are: ways of producing and hence also mastering "the world" and then passing it on (as fact) to others—even if such ontological production is to be dressed in the language of immanence and autopoiesis. (My suspicion towards ontology does not mean I do not believe there are "things" out there beyond the realm of the human and beyond the human conceptualization of them. However, as soon as the human takes to the human-centric practice of philosophizing, "things" immediately become far less objective, realist and "out there" than this human would often like, or would like others to believe.)

The reflections offered in this short book are linked to my previous work on what it means to live a good life at a time when the very notion of life is undergoing a radical reformulation, both on a philosophical and biotechnological level. However, I am less concerned here with a critical discussion of different theoretical positions on ethics and more with sketching out an affirmative proposal for an ethics that *makes sense*—and that *senses its own making*. This idea of the ethical call of the universe, in its temporary stabilizations, expands on my argument from *Bioethics in the Age of New Media*, in which I positioned bioethics as an originary philosophy, situated even before ontology. That idea was inspired by the work of Emmanuel Levinas, although I was—and still am—troubled by the humanist limitations of Levinas' ethics, whereby primordial responsibility exerted upon me always comes from human others. In bioethics as an "ethics of life" the way I understand it, the human self has to respond to an expanded set of obligations that affect her, make an impression on her, allow for her differentiation from the world around her and demand a response that is not just a reaction. While I do recognize, together with other theorists of post-anthropocentric thought, that "it is not all about us",[2] I also acknowledge the singular human responsibility which is exercised both by philosophical theory (which is consciously undertaken by few) and by philosophical practice (which is a much more widespread undertaking, even if not always a conscious one). This recognition hopefully justifies to some extent the reluctant yet also sometimes inevitable use of the pronoun "I" throughout this volume, and the multiple paradoxes implied in any attempt on the part of a singular female human writer to author a post-anthropocentric ethics. The post-anthropocentric ethics of expanded obligations becomes a way of taking responsibility, by the human, for various sorts of thickenings of the universe, across different scales, and of responding to the tangled mesh of everyday connections and relations. To do this, I shall go back to Levinas for inspiration, but also cross-pollinate him with other ideas with the help of some Brilliant Bees: (Henri) Bergson, (Karen) Barad, (Rosi) Braidotti, (Wendy) Brown and (Jane) Bennett, as well as some other members of the Philosophical Hive Mind (Tom Cohen, Claire Colebrook, Gilles Deleuze, Jacques Derrida, Donna Haraway, Tim Ingold, Stanisław Lem and Timothy Morton).

If the mode of working in this book embraces a post-masculinist rationality, its method—in a departure from a modernist form of critique—can be loosely described as "critical vitalism". This method involves rethinking and remaking "life" and what we can do with it. Taking life as a (yet) non-valorized minimal condition, critical vitalism remains attuned to stoppages in life, seeing life as both a becoming and a fracturing process. Claire Colebrook articulates this dual, productive-destructive tendency of life, in the following terms: "Philosophy cannot simply decide to begin from ground zero; nor can the living being become so open and receptive to its milieu that it would not inflect, pervert or fold its passions around its own life. Immanence is an ongoing struggle, and the aims of becoming-imperceptible, seeing the world anew or becoming-child are given force and power just through the resistances they encounter" (2010: 166). Critical vitalism entails knowing the difference of difference. It considers how differences ensue and matter, who they matter to, how matter resists and recoils, and to what effect. Starting from the premise that "everything is interconnected" (Morton 2010: 1), it also considers differentiation within those processes of connectivity while offering a reflection on human situatedness in and responsibility for different connections of relations of which s/he is part. Situated at the crossroads of cultural theory, media and cultural studies, continental philosophy and art, the book inscribes itself in the trajectory of what Timothy Morton has called "the ecological thought". Yet, still following Morton, this is a curious kind of ecology, as it is not based on any prelapsarian, romanticized notion of Nature that can allegedly be recouped in order to make the world and our lives in it better.

Let me explain at last what it thus means for the ethical framework outlined here to be pointed, via the preposition "for" included in the book's title, towards the geo-historical period described as "the Anthropocene". Proposed by the Dutch chemist Paul Crutzen in 2000, the term "Anthropocene" (from *anthropo*, man, and *cene*, new) serves as a name for a new geological epoch that supposedly follows the Holocene, "the epoch that began at the end of the last ice age, 11,700 years ago, and that—officially, at least—continues to this day" (Kolbert 29). The need for the new term is being justified by the fact that human influence upon the geo- and biosphere via processes such as farming, deforestation, mining and urbanization, to name but a few, has been so immense that it actually merits a new designation in order to address the challenges raised by that influence. Even though the term has not been universally and unquestioningly adopted by all geologists, its use has significantly increased over the last decade—and has been popularized beyond the professional scientific community thanks to the 2011 article on the topic by Elizabeth Kolbert in the *National Geographic* magazine. Yet even amongst those who are sympathetic to the term there is widespread doubt as to which moment in time should serve as a beginning of this epoch: some point to the early days of agriculture some 8,000 years ago, others to the Industrial Revolution or to the last fifty years of excessive consumption, while still others see the Anthropocene as an epoch that is yet to come.

Significantly, in the opening pages of his *Ecological Thought* Morton claims that "One of the things that modern society has damaged, along with ecosystems and species and the global climate, is thinking" (4). The Anthropocene can therefore perhaps be seen as articulating, alongside the ecological disasters, this crisis of critical thinking. My own use of the term "Anthropocene" in this book is first and foremost as an ethical pointer rather than as a scientific descriptor. In other words, the Anthropocene serves here as a designation of the human obligation towards the geo- and biosphere, but also towards thinking about the geo- and biosphere *as concepts*. The ethics for the Anthropocene would therefore entail a call for a return to critical thinking, for a reparation of thought. Combining inventiveness with criticality, it would promote non-instrumental modes of thinking, while avoiding easy solutionism and what some theorists have called the derangement of scale (see Clark; Kember and Zylinska), whereby filling in half a kettle is perceived as "doing one's bit for the environment". Yet, even if the Anthropocene is about "the age of man", the ethical thinking it designates is strongly post-anthropocentric, as indicated earlier, in the sense that it does not consider the human to be the dominant or the most important species, nor does is see the world as arranged solely for human use and benefit. The term does however entail an appeal to human singularity (not to be confused with human supremacy), coupled with a recognition that we can make a difference to the ongoing dynamic processes taking in the biosphere and the geosphere—of which we are part.

Minimal ethics for the Anthropocene is not just an updated form of environmental ethics: it does not pivot on any coherent notion of an "environment" (or, as mentioned earlier, "nature") as an identifiable entity but rather concerns itself with dynamic relations between entities across various scales such as stem cells, flowers, dogs, humans, rivers, electricity pylons, computer networks, and planets, to name but a few. This is why the closest way of describing this kind of minimal ethics would be as an ethics of life, with life understood both philosophically and biologically. Its starting premise is that we humans are making a difference to the arrangements of what we are calling "the world". Naturally, we are not the only or even the most important actors that are making such a difference. It would be extremely naive and short-sighted to assume that, as it would be to proclaim that we can affect or control all occurrences within that world—but we are perhaps uniquely placed to turn the making of such difference into an ethical task. Thanks to our human ability to tell stories and to philosophize, we can not only grasp the deep historical stratification of values through an involvement in what Gilles Deleuze and Félix Guattari called "a geology of morals" (1987) but also work out possibilities for making better differences across various scales. While our participation in the differentiation of matter is ongoing, frequently collective or distributed, and often unconscious, ethics names a situation when those processes of differentiation are accounted for—when they occur as a cognitive-affective effort to rearrange the solidified moral strata, with a view to producing a better geo-moral landscape.

The ethics discussed here is minimal in the sense that it is non-systemic (i.e., it does not remain rooted in any large conceptual system) and non-normative (which is to say, it does not rest on any fixed prior values, nor does it postulate any firm values in the process). Inevitably, for some readers a non-normative ethics will be a non sequitur, a conceptual blind alley that will not deliver what it promises. For me, in turn, non-normativity is the only possible way of thinking ethics and life generally in a responsible and non-hubristic way, from amidst life itself. But, wary of capital-V values, I nevertheless embark on this project with one minimal assumption: a conviction that we have a responsibility to engage with life—materially and conceptually—because, as we know from Socrates, "the unexamined life is not worth living" (Plato *Apology*, 38a, non-pag.). What counts as the examination of life goes beyond the Socratic method of inquiry instantiated between two parties with a view to eliminating erroneous hypotheses. It also involves physicalist engagement with the matter of life, with its particles and unfoldings.

The minimalism of the ethics project presented in this book does not just refer to the premises of its main argument but also to its content. Aimed as an exercise in brevity, the book adopts a formal structure that comprises ten short essays, each one presenting one argument or proposition. The aim here is to say *just enough*. The book also contains a photographic project, *Topia daedala*, which arises out of ongoing efforts on my part to "do philosophy" with different media. While the project draws on selected philosophical standpoints, as well some ideas from physics, biology, neuroscience, sociology, anthropology, and cultural and media theory, academic references have been kept brief. The argument is constructed on the basis of a spiral, with ideas being introduced across the subsequent theses and then returned to and expanded on. Linear reading may be one way of getting through the book. Yet, given that each chapter constitutes a small essay in it its own right, entering the book at any point may offer a different reading experience, introducing the reader to this minimal ethics *in medias res*.

In medias res can actually serve as a description of the location of our minimal ethics.

Notes

1. The book arose from a successful lecture-play at the Royal Court in London in which Emmott took part in the summer of 2012.

2. This is a frequent mantra of various theorists of post-anthropocentric thought, principally the followers of actor-network theory and object-oriented ontology: it is even included in the dedication of Levi R. Bryant's *The Democracy of Objects*.

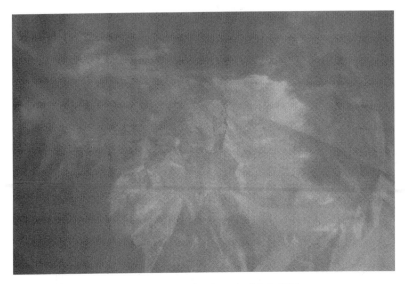

Fig. 3: Joanna Zylinska, *Topia daedala* 3, 2014

Chapter 2

Scale

The minimal ethics posited in this book needs to be thought on a universal scale. This may sound like a paradox, yet it will only seem so if we rush ahead of ourselves and expect such ethics to furnish us with some generally applicable principles that will have to remain valid across all times and locales. But we have said nothing of the kind. By speaking of the universal scale we are merely attempting to situate our philosophical endeavors meaningfully and responsibly, without foreclosing them all too early by the kind of thinking that would carve out entities such as "the animal", "the body" and "the gene", and locations such as "the world", "Africa" and "the lab", and then attempt to work out good ways of managing relations between them. The universal starting point assumes the shared materiality of the universe, which is another way of saying that everything is made of the same stuff— although not necessarily in the same way. And yet, as explained by Stephen W. Hawking, "Despite the fact that the universe is so uniform and homogeneous on a large scale, it contains local irregularities, such as stars and galaxies. These are thought to have developed from small differences in the density of the early universe from one region to another" (122). The preceding statements already posit this somewhat imaginary entity, the universe, which includes planets, galaxies and the space between them, or, putting it differently, all matter and energy that exists, or that is actively transmuting and interrelating. The universe thus serves as a fictitious point of unity for an ongoing process of the unfolding of matter across time and space that supposedly started around 13.82 billion years ago, with an event we have retrospectively called "the Big Bang". (Even though ongoing, this process will one day come to a halt. There could have also been other events and processes before the Big Bang, but we do not know anything about them.)

The term "scale", from Latin *scala*, means "ladder": it is a practical and conceptual device that allows us to climb up and down various spatiotemporal dimensions in order to see things from different viewpoints. Adopting a universal scale is therefore inevitably a dynamic process. It involves coming to terms with time understood, after Bergson, as "duration", a continuous flow into which we as observers make insertions in order to carve out some "solids" from it, to temporarily stabilize matter into entities. In an attempt to grasp the passage of time, we make incisions in it with our proprioceptive and cognitive apparatuses, and then pass off the products of these incisions as images of the world. Bringing (back) the universal scale will thus serve as a reminder for us that there is an excess to our acts of world-making and that it is perhaps imprudent or even irresponsible to forget about it in all kinds of discussions—those concerning politics,

ethics or even our everyday existence. Timothy Clark
points out that considerations of scale tend to under-
mine many policies, concepts and common-sense
beliefs about what we refer to as "our world", since any
efforts to conduct environmental reform in one coun-
try, say, may be effectively negated by the lack of any
such efforts in many other (frequently more powerful, wealthier and more environmentally damaging)
locations of the globe. This forgetting of scale results
in what Clark calls "a derangement of linguistic and
intellectual proportion", whereby filling the kettle with
just enough water to make tea or buying a slightly less
petrol-guzzling make of car are seen as ways of "saving
the planet". Yet it is not only many eco-activists and,
more broadly, those who care about the environment
and climate change, that suffer from this kind of scalar derangement. The latter malady also affects many
scholars in the humanities, including those occupying themselves with problems of ethics and morality.
Adopting a similarly mechanistic approach to this pre-
sumed entity they alternatively call "the planet" and
"the world", humanities thinkers of various theoretical
persuasions in various disciplines first posit and locate
this entity at a distance, and then try to *act on* it. This
leads Clark to conclude that "dominant modes of lit-
erary and cultural criticism are blind to scale effects
in ways that now need to be addressed" (150). The
problem with this "planetary" mode of thinking lies in
the *apparent* grasping of complexity, which is nothing
more but a form of reductionism, whereby "[r]eceived
concepts of agency, rationality and responsibility
are being strained or even begin to fall apart into a

bewildering generalizing of the political that can make even filling a kettle as public an act as voting" (151). My attempt to outline a *minimal* ethics thought across a universal scale offers a partial response to Clark's exhortation to consider scale effects seriously.

The preceding argument hopefully explains to some extent why the minimal ethics outlined in this book needs to work on a universal scale. Once again, this is not to say that such ethics needs to be *applicable* across all times and locales: it just needs to acknowledge the temporally and spatially unbound perspective of "the universe" that circumscribes how relations, entities and phenomena appear *to us*. It also confirms *our* specific locatedness in space and time from which we will conduct our enquiry. If we then continue to philosophize, proselytize or moralize about the world, we will have registered that we are doing it from a uniquely situated (even if inherently unstable) standpoint, on a certain selected, historically legitimized scale. Bringing back universality, which is a form of McLuhanian "all-at-onceness",[3] as a horizon of our enquiry can therefore actually act as a reminder to us of the partiality of a story we can tell, or of an intervention we can make—but also of the locatedness of the many concepts and values we humans have developed across all kinds of constrained historical scales. An attempt to grasp a phenomenon as complex as, say, climate change across various scales may lead to a challenge "to basic dominant assumptions about the nature and seeming self-evident value of 'democracy' as the most enlightened way to conduct human affairs" (Clark 152). Thinking at scales that intuitively used to "make sense" may actually turn out to be, according to Clark, "a form of intellectual and ethical containment. [...] Viewed on very long time scales, human history and culture can take on unfamiliar shapes, [...] altering conceptions of what makes something 'important' and what does not. Nonhuman entities take on a decisive agency" (159). Acknowledging this means being called to reconsider our notions of politics and ethics beyond the conventional liberal and human/ist bounds and templates—in the light of the recognition that "it is not all about us"—even if the act of theorizing and reflecting on such politics and ethics itself is to remain, at least for the time being, a uniquely human task.

An invitation to look at things on a universal scale is also meant as an encouragement for us to swap the telescope for the microscope,[4] to change perspective from the universal to the quantum, in order to try and see otherwise—without losing sight of the complex entanglements of matter, and us *as matter*, across various ways, and of the fact that we are not really able to "see" much at either end of the physical spectrum. The notion of entanglement is used here in the specific sense given to it by Karen Barad, for whom "Existence is not an individual affair". According to Barad, "Individuals do not preexist their interactions; rather, individuals emerge through and as part of their entangled intra-relating" (ix). From this perspective, the notion of scale cannot be seen as an external measuring stick that can be objectively applied to time and space but is rather part of the phenomena it attempts to measure, as "time and space, like matter and

meaning, come into existence, are iteratively recon-
figured through each intra-action, thereby making
it impossible to differentiate in any absolute sense
between creation and renewal, beginning and return-
ing, continuity and discontinuity" (ix). The ontology of the world is therefore that of entanglement. It
entails the constant unfolding of matter across time—
but also a temporary stabilization of matter into
entities (or rather, things "we" and other nonhuman
"beings" recognize as entities) in order to execute certain acts and perform certain tasks. Only very few of
these acts will be pre-planned and conscious. Yet it is
precisely this perhaps rather narrow domain of at least
partly conscious activity undertaken by entangled
beings who have historically allocated to themselves
the name "humans" that becomes a field of action for
the minimal ethics outlined here.

This mode of thinking on a universal scale might
seem to be seamlessly and unproblematically aligned
with other modes of "big thinking" currently en
vogue, such as big history or ubiquitous computing.
Yet, in their upscaling and downscaling efforts, the
latter approaches more often than not turn out to be
just *not deep enough* because they overlook too much
in the process. This is why Sarah Kember and I, in our
article "Media Always and Everywhere: A Cosmic
Approach", have drawn on a principle that postulates
the "just right" size or amount to be applied in each
particular case, while not losing sight of the wider horizon. Called "the Goldilocks principle", this thought
device is used in fields such as computing, biology or
economics to suggest that a given phenomenon needs

to remain within certain margins and avoid reaching extremes. The term is developed from a children's story "The Three Bears", in which a little girl named Goldilocks sneaks into a house inhabited by three furry creatures, trying to make herself comfortable in it. On identifying the "just right" porridge, chair and bed, the trespassing little proto-feminist is made to face the irate bears, who chase her away from their house. For Kember and me, Goldilocks inscribes itself in the long line of feminist figurations such as "the cyborg" or "the nomad" proposed by thinkers such as Donna Haraway and Rosi Braidotti.[5] The cyborg and the nomad tread foreign territories as uninvited guests with a view to outlining an alternative political imaginary. The role of Goldilocks in thinking on the universal scale is to make us aware of our own derangements when sliding up and down the historical or even geological pole all too smoothly, to recognize some blockages on it, and to add some stoppage points herself. It is therefore to provide a "just right" assessment of universality.

A Goldilocks-controlled universality can help us enact the post-masculinist rationality mentioned in the first chapter, which is a form of rationality that, in acknowledging the multiscalar properties of the universe, eschews any attempts to collapse those scales in order to tell a totalizing story about it. A minimal ethics thus envisaged is thus inevitably a form of pragmatics. It involves recognizing, as well as undertaking, pragmatic temporary stabilizations of time and matter. Minimal ethical statements can be understood as articulations, from Latin *articulatio* ("separation into joints"), as they both link things together and enact a separation between them in order to say something about the relations of the world, and about our possible modest contribution to developing and managing those relations. Ethical articulations therefore always perform an ontological function: they stabilize and organize the universe for us, but in a way that is to benefit not just us but also *the universe as such*. It is in this sense that ethics precedes ontology: not on a linear scale but rather in the sense of making a prior demand on us.

Seeing things across different scales is more than an attempt to represent the universe: it actively produces entities and relations. It is in this sense that seeing is already a "doing" (Barad 51), with concepts being understood as "specific physical arrangements", not "mere ideations" (54). Such an approach makes of theorizing "an embodied practice, rather than a spectator sport of matching linguistic representations to pre-existing things" (Barad 54). Consequently, the minimal ethics I am outlining here needs to be an embedded and embodied practice; it needs to involve a material working out of the relations between entities and of their varying forces, instead of relying on a priori *systemic* normativity. True to its name though, it does adopt some minimal principles, the first one of which is the recognition of the entangled positioning of the human in, or rather with, the universe and a uniquely human responsibility for that universe. That responsibility is also minimal, in the sense that it does not involve any pre-decided values and rules. It only carries an injunction to mobilize the human faculties of reasoning and sensing, and of articulating thoughts and affects through the historically outlined practice of philosophy (or, more specifically, ethics as a practice of both value formation and reflection on it), in order to respond to the processes and relations of the universe—some of which may directly involve the human. This inherent connectedness of the universe should not be understood as "linkages among preexisting nested scales but as the agential enfolding of different scales through one another (so that, for example, the different scales of individual bodies, homes, communities, regions, nations, and the global are not seen as geometrically nested in accordance with some physical notion of size but rather are understood as being intra-actively produced through one another)" (Barad 245). The notion of intra-action—as opposed to the concept of "interaction", which assumes an encounter before previously stabilized entities— points to the inherent dynamism of matter, which only "becomes something" in relation to something else, over and over again. Naturally, the majority of such intra-actions across different scales are beyond human ken. Minimal ethics refers precisely to this very narrow spectrum of the universe's intra-actions for which the human is able to take at least some degree of responsibility—materially, conceptually and morally. It is this partial *ability to do this*, rather than a prior resolution of *how to do it*, that serves as a tiny corner-pebble of our minimal ethics for the Anthropocene.

Notes

3. "Today, the instantaneous world of electric information media involves all of us, all at once. Ours is a brand-new world of all-at-oneness. Time, in a sense, has ceased and space has vanished", McLuhan on McLuhanism, WNDT Educational Broadcasting Network, 1966.

4. "Gazing out into the night sky or deep down into the structure of matter, with telescope or microscope in hand, Man reconfirms his ability to negotiate immense differences in scale in the blink of an eye. Designed specifically for our visual apparatus, telescopes and microscopes are the stuff of mirrors, reflecting what is out there. Nothing is too vast or too minute. Though a mere speck, a blip on the radar screen of all that is, Man is the center around which the world turns. Man is the sun, the nucleus, the fulcrum, the unifying force, the glue that holds it all together. Man is an individual apart from all the rest. And it is this very distinction that bestows on him the inheritance of distance, a place from which to reflect—on the world, his fellow man, and himself. A distinct individual, the unit of all measure, finitude made flesh, his separateness is the key. Representationalism, metaphysical individualism, and humanism work hand in hand, holding this worldview in place. These forces have such a powerful grip on contemporary patterns of thought that even some of the most concerted efforts to escape the grasp of these anthropocentric forces have failed" (Barad 134).

5. See Haraway, *Simians, Cyborgs and Women* and Braidotti, *Nomadic Subjects.*

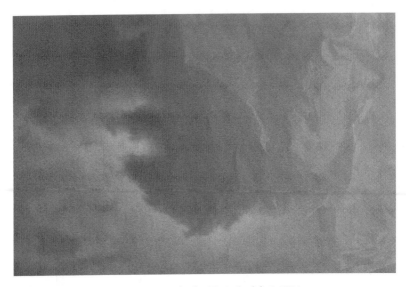

Fig. 4: Joanna Zylinska, *Topia daedala* 4, 2014

Chapter 3

Process

There has been a tendency in recent years amongst cultural theorists of various ilk to speak about process and relationality as the dominant modes of capturing the unstable ontology of what we conventionally refer to as "the world". So-called process philosophy, expounded by thinkers such as Friedrich Nietzsche, Gilles Deleuze or A.N. Whitehead, foregrounds change as the key aspects of the becoming of the matter of the world—and of our becoming material in the world. The world itself, as we will discuss later on, is seen here as nothing more than a temporary mental organization, undertaken by the spatially embedded and embodied human, of the various processes of which this human is part. Process philosophy postulates what could be described as a "fluid ontology", where being is not defined through substances with their supposedly inherent and immutable properties but is rather seen as dynamic and constantly changing. Even though the roots of process philosophy can be traced back to the ideas of the Greek philosopher Heraclitus, with his theory of the universal flux, this philosophical framework has always constituted a more marginal line of thinking within the Western epistemic edifice. Yet processual thinking has recently gained a new lease of life through its (not always unproblematic) encounters with scientific developments in quantum physics, cosmology and molecular biology, developments that point to the inherent instability and changeability of the universe at both particle and cosmic level. The growing interest in process philosophy can be seen as an attempt to overcome the inherent bias of Western metaphysics, which has shaped many static concepts and assumptions that underpin our language and worldview.

The argument developed in this book remains aligned with the processual mode of thinking about what our language traditionally describes as "reality", but it also stays attuned to the possible disruptions to the flow of life encapsulated by this framework—even if it does not go all the way towards replacing the processual framework with a (so-called) object-oriented one. Yet it is these disruptions to the process that, first, allow us to see the process *as a process*, and, second, that make the process interesting as an event. It is precisely through these disruptions that life gets temporarily stabilized, that it presents itself *to us* as a series of states and objects. Many process philosophers do in fact acknowledge that "there are temporally stable and reliably recurrent aspects of reality. But they take such aspects of persistence to be the regular behavior of dynamic organizations that arise due to the continuously ongoing interaction of processes" (Seibt non-pag.). It is important to recognize that these temporary stabilizations, which can be described as *cuts made to the flow of life*, occur both at the level of matter and (human) mind. Some of these cuts are, to use Karen Barad's term, "agential", which is to say they enact "a resolution within the phenomenon of the inherent ontological (and semantic) indeterminacy" (140)—although not all of these agential cuts have a corresponding human agent that enacts them. The recognition of the outcomes of those cuts is an epistemological activity: this is how we make sense, cognitively and affectively, of the chaos of the world. The act of taking responsibility for those, perhaps rare, cuts which we humans are capable of enacting (or not enacting) is in turn what I am defining throughout this book as an ethical endeavor.

Henri Bergson is one of the process philosophers who can be of help to us in getting to grips with the process-entity dualism. His *Creative Evolution* is an attempt to encourage us to overcome the fossilized habits of our mind. The mind inevitably spatializes time by cutting its flow into what he calls solids, thus making us miss out on the true essence of life, or what we might call its lifeness. Indeed, for Bergson, our intellect is unable to grasp true duration because it is only at home working on inert matter, but the flow of time requires us to adjust its somewhat mechanical working (169). "If our existence were composed of separate states with an impassive ego to unite them, for us there would be no duration", writes Bergson (6). Bergson's philosophy of time is therefore primarily intuitive or, we might even say, experiential, a point he articulates in his restatement of the Heraclitean river dilemma: "consciousness cannot go through the same state twice" (8). For Bergson, time and duration provide the organizing logic of the universe, a thought he expresses as follows: "the truth is that we change without ceasing, and that the state itself is nothing but change" (4). To deal with this incessant duration, we need to turn to intuition to recapture a more instinctual way of grasping life that allows us to apprehend that which is in process. Yet Bergson's observation that "No doubt, it is useful to us, in view of our ulterior manipulation, to regard each object as divisible into parts arbitrarily cut up, each part being again divisible as we like, and so on ad infinitum" (169-70) signals a certain inevitable if reluctant pragmatism entailed in his argument, one that brings up states even if in order to debunk them.

The differentiation between process and entity is itself premised on the possibility of the human stepping outside the world she is describing in order to say something about it. However, this is not to say that process is all that is. It is rather to recognize that "process" and "entity" are terms we humans use to describe, however clumsily, the different speeds and scales at which the transformations of matter are taking place in the universe—and to acknowledge that these transformations matter to us humans in different ways. Derrida makes a similar point when replying to Bernard Stiegler in *Echographies of Television* in their discussion of the technical process and what it involves (incidentally, for Stiegler as much as for Derrida, *techne* is originary to life, including human life, rather than being a mere product of human activity). Derrida says: "to speak of a technical process, and indeed of its acceleration, mustn't lead us to overlook the fact that this flux, even if it picks up speed, none-theless passes through *determined* phases and struc-tures" (76). He is concerned with the way the term "process" tends to be used as a "pretext for saying: It's a flow, a continuous development; there is *nothing but* process" (76). Consistent with the deconstruc-tive logic that shapes his philosophical endeavor, one that shows seemingly opposing terms as each other's conditions of possibility when they emerge as part of our human discourse in the shape of tools that help us make sense of the world, Derrida insists: "No, there is not *only* process. Or at least, process always includes stases, states, halts" (76). This kind of argument has been branded "correlationist" by Quentin Meillassoux and other proponents of the recently fashionable spec-ulative realism, in the sense that humans are seem-ingly unable to envisage the world in isolation from themselves and their own concerns. Yet this is nothing of the kind. The world (or rather what we are calling the world) does of course unfold and act in a myriad ways outside and beyond us, many of which we are unable to see, experience and grasp. However, for us to be able to say anything about it, to engage in any kind of philosophizing, we are at the same time bring-ing forth this world in a necessarily cut-up, solidified and inadequate way, for which we furnish ourselves with concepts such as adequacy and truth in order to assess our efforts, as well as efforts of those whose modes of thinking are not aligned with our own. Many seem oblivious of this fact, engaging instead as they do in the construction of ontological edifices that float like palaces in the sky—and then passing them off as descriptions of reality on to others.

The linguistic acrobatics we are inevitably engaged in here go beyond a mere exercise in representationalism or metaphor-production. In his reading of Bergson's use of concepts, John Mullarkey points out that "if the language of process corresponds to process-reality that is because it also *proceeds as a process-reality*, rather than because it is a static image of it" (154; emphasis added). In other words, language does not so much attempt to (and fail to attempt to) capture life but rather enacts it, for us humans, in a certain way. The distinction between process and entity is therefore a heuristic, a conceptual device that helps us grasp the world and respond to it, while at the same time moving in it and being moved by it. The distinction is therefore both an ontological cut and an ethical device. Taking on the role of an injunction, it calls on us humans to respond to the movement that carries us through the world. Significantly, for Tim Ingold humans do not live *in* the world but rather move *through* it. He uses the term "wayfaring" to describe "the embodied experience of this perambulatory movement" (2011: 148). Movement is also a way of getting to know the world, according to Ingold, where knowledge is not seen as classificatory but rather as "storied", being constantly "under construction" (159). Indeed, he goes so far as to suggest that movement itself "is knowing" (160), challenging in this way the rigid taxonomies we construct about the world and thus foreclose it, make it lifeless, or—to cite Bergson—"solid".

How can this more intuitive mode of engaging with the world help us in our ethical project in
the Anthropocene era? Should we try and intuit the
Anthropocene and ways of responding to it rather than
try to theorize it? Counterintuitive as it may sound,
this is perhaps the only sensible way of approaching
the issue of the human's intervention into the geo-
and bio-sphere since many well-documented rational arguments and responses have either completely
failed or, deep down, have been completely irrational.
And thus the popular Al Gore documentary about
global warming, *An Inconvenient Truth* (2006), originally devised as a slide presentation, may have raised
awareness of its viewers but it is more difficult to
prove it has actually changed behavior, especially on
any meaningful scale. Any individual efforts to recycle more and switch off unnecessary lights have been
more than offset by transnational counter-efforts: for
example, "[i]n 2012 the US energy company Exxon—
the world's largest oil producer—signed a deal with
Russia to invest up to $500 billion in oil and gas
exploration and extraction in the Arctic, in Russia's
Kara Sea" (Emmott non-pag.), while around that time
the UK government issued nearly 200 new licenses
to drill for gas and oil in the North Sea. Suggestions
to repair the environmental damage by only filling
in half of the kettle, using one rather than two sheets
of toilet paper, or buying an electric car fail precisely
due to the inability to distinguish between process
and entity and to think across different scales without
collapsing them into a (singular) human measure of
things. Such suggestions position environmental and

climate change as a matter of individual moral decisions one is obliged to take, while completely blanking out the scale of phenomena we are facing, phenomena such as the overexploitation of oceans, the loss of tropical rainforests and woodlands, the rise in atmospheric brown clouds as a result of wood burning and oil use, and the overconsumption of water (including so-called "hidden water", i.e., water used to produce other things) and meat.[6] Even the generic call for the protection of life is misguided, even if well-intentioned, because it, somewhat hubristically, turns life into an object, one that needs protection and that is posited as separated from us humans so that *we* can offer *it* protection, while equipping us with a God-like fantasy that we can indeed control and regulate it. In a truly Bergsonian vein, Ingold argues that

> An understanding of the unity of life in terms of genealogical relatedness is bought at the cost of cutting out every single organism from the relational matrix in which it lives and grows. In this understanding, life presents itself to our awareness not as the interlaced meshwork, famously invoked by Charles Darwin in his image of the "entangled bank" (Darwin 1950: 64, see Chapter 6, p. 84), but rather as an immense scheme of classification—nowadays going by the name of "biodiversity"—in which every individual is assigned to a specific taxon (species, genus) on the basis of covert attributes, comprising the genotype, that it is

deemed to possess in advance of their phe-
notypic expression in a real-world environment (Ingold 2000a: 217). (2011: 163)

A minimal injunction for our ethics of the
Anthropocene would not therefore call on those of us
who call ourselves human to protect "life" at all cost
but rather to recognize that life itself is a system constituted by a dynamic movement of forces, that time
itself is movement, that we are just wayfarers in the
world, and that microbes were there before us (see
Eldredge) and will no doubt survive us. Such ethics
may seem terribly ineffective but, given the ineffec-
tivity of the more grandiose sounding programs and
undertakings as described above, perhaps a modest experiment in reimagining life—and in thinking
and living critically—can actually be seen as a viable
and vital alternative? This recognition of wayfaring
as a critical model of engaging otherwise involves
acknowledging, with Lynn Margulis, that "Neither
animal nor plant is an eternal category of classifica-
tion" (56), that "Animals and plants are far more similar to each other than they are to all the other kinds
of Earth life" (56) and, last but not least, that extinction as a form of movement is part and parcel of
the process.

   This recognition does not have to amount to fatalism: it carries a task for us transient human animals
to start figuring out ways of moving better, of dying
better, and of becoming extinct better, while not losing sight of the fact that any notion of "goodness"
with regard to life is always species-specific and hence

inevitably antagonistic towards its other articulations and enactments across other scales. Minimal ethics can therefore be said to refer loosely to a set of actions we can undertake once we have intuitively grasped this constant movement of life, of which we are part, and then turned to our compromised and imperfect faculty of reason—which is perhaps primarily a story-telling faculty—in order to tell better stories about life in the universe, and about life (and death) *of* the universe. Read on an evolutionary non-anthropocentric scale, extinction is an inevitable process of the withering away of any species, a process against which human attempts to "adapt better" must look hubristically naive. If the human cannot armor himself against extinction, its looming prospect "opens up the question of life more generally, and of how we wish to live whatever time is left for the human species" (Colebrook 2012: non-pag.). Evolution and extinction therefore open up the question of ethics.

Notes

6. For more on these issues see Timothy Clark, "Derangements of Scale" and Stephen Emmott, *Ten Billion*.

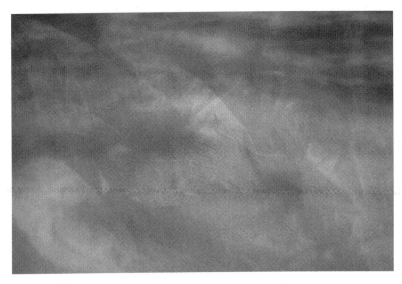

Fig. 5: Joanna Zylinska, *Topia daedala* 5, 2014

Chapter 4

Evolution

This chapter provides some further historical and intellectual context for the ethical project undertaken in this book. It is through the story of evolution—understood as both narrative and fact, as the unfolding of history as well as the very possibility of history—that the contextualization of minimal ethics will take place in what follows. The problem of context is important, partly because contextualization is something that any pragmatic approach to ethics must embark upon and partly because "there is nothing outside context" (Derrida 1988: 136).[7] This latter statement does not indicate that our minimal ethics will be relativist, as contextualization is simply inevitable. In other words, there can be no ethics that would remain separate from the context in which it operates, even if, or *especially if* this ethics is to be thought across different scales. This act of pragmatic recognition requires us to abandon any fantasy of speaking about universally applicable truths, values and morals. Such things simply do not exist, and indeed cannot exist— although there are many dispensers of morality who try to persuade us otherwise. Paradoxical as it may sound, a call to consider things across different scales is an attempt to avoid any kind of universalization of ethics, and to acknowledge the limitations of the human worldview. In other words, we must recognize that the human only ever carves out small sections of the universe, a process through which s/he produces ideas and entities. Overcoming the presumption that "man is the measure of all things", minimal ethics—which we have termed post-anthropocentric, or (after Karen Barad and Rosi Braidotti), posthumanist—will not be "held captive to the distance scale of the human" but will rather remain "attentive to the practices by which scale is produced" (Barad 136). The imperative to engage, materially and conceptually—although inevitably in a way that is restricted by our locatedness in a tiny section of space-time—with scalar processes and effects across the universe is therefore the first condition of minimal ethics. This is precisely what I mean when I say that this ethics needs to be *thought on a universal scale*, even if it itself will remain *decidedly non-universalist*.

One major issue that the question of scale requires us to rethink in our interrogation of human ontology and human history is the differentiation between biology and culture upon which the division between sciences and humanities has been premised. Yet the main source of the problem is not so much the conflation of the cultural with the biological, as explained by Tim Ingold in his article "Beyond Biology and Culture: The Meaning of Evolution in a Relational World", but rather the reduction of the biological to the genetic, a mode of thinking that still informs modern evolutionary theory. Even though the majority of biologists are wary of the charge of genetic reductionism, they still hold on to the notion of "a *complex interaction* of 'biological' and 'cultural' factors, operating in a given environment" (Ingold 2004: 217). What we are faced with here are two sets of ontologically different processes and entities, with biological factors seen as genetically transmitted and cultural ones supposedly transmitted by imitation or social learning. Biology thus ends up being tied to genes after all.[8] The work of critical biologists such as Susan Oyama, Richard Lewontin or Daniel Lehrman has raised some serious questions for the stability of the dichotomy between nature *and* nurture, "as though these were separate things— genes on the one hand, environment on the other— that then interact to form the organism" (Ingold 2004: 218). Following Lehrman, Ingold points out that any such interactions occur not between genes and environment bur rather between organism and environment, whereby the organism is "the continually changing embodiment of a whole history of previous interactions that have shaped its life course", while the environment "exists only in relation to the organisms that inhabit it, and embodies a history of interactions with them" (218).

We are introduced here to a much more processual and relational way of thinking about the world, whereby matter stabilizes into "organisms" which nevertheless always remain entangled with their "environment". If the process of organismic differentiation is continuous, the organism needs to be seen not as an entity but as multiple processes of entanglement, a temporally unfolding set of relations that keep making and unmaking the topological boundaries. This brings us to a conceptualization of life as "the creative potential of a dynamic field of relationships in which specific beings emerge and take the forms they do, each in relation to the others. In that sense, life is not so much *in* organisms as organisms *in* life" (Ingold 2004: 219). Arguably, such a mode of thinking was already at work in Darwin's early theory of evolution but, in its later incarnations, such as Henry Spencer's theory of "natural selection" as encapsulated by the concept of the "survival of the fittest" (later evident in the instrumentalism of evolutionary biology), it became translated into a linear force with a set of predesigned tasks to accomplish. Bergson's 1907 book *Creative Evolution* was an attempt to counter such a teleological and instrumentalist reading of evolution. The ongoing engagement with Bergsonian thought in contemporary humanities may be seen to be inspired by a desire to recapture that forgotten vitality of life.

As explained in the previous chapter, Bergson's argument in *Creative Evolution* is premised on the critique of the human intellect. Rather than seeing it as a pinnacle of evolutionary development, he positions the intellect as a fossilized product of evolution that is structurally incapable "of presenting the true nature of life, the full meaning of the evolutionary movement in the course of its way", and thus a regression as much as a progression (xx). Bergson justifies his conclusion by explaining that the intellect deals only with "solids", temporarily stabilized images and concepts of the world which we take for the latter's true states and their representations. However, on taking cognizance of them, we are simultaneously overlooking the wider background, or we could say *context*: that of duration and of life's continuous unfolding. This is why Bergson encourages us to turn to intuition, a mode of apprehending the world which bridges instinctual actions and reactions with our habits of thought in order to recapture what the intellect has banned us from experiencing. If "matter has a tendency to constitute *isolable* systems, that can be treated geometrically", Bergson acknowledges that this is *just* a tendency, since matter "does not go to the end, and the isolation is never complete" (13). Reconnecting the intellect back to intuition can help us experience the vibrant vitality of matter, its ongoing dynamism and productivity. He goes on to argue that "[t]he universe *endures*", which means that by studying the nature of time we shall comprehend that "duration means invention, the creation of forms, the continual elaboration of the absolutely new" (14). It is in this sense that evolution for Bergson is creative rather than pre-planned and mechanistic.

In the light of the preceding argument with regard to the ongoing duration of the universe, we can see biology and culture as mutually entangled processes that differ in degree, but not in kind, to use Bergsonian terminology. A similar view has been embraced by proponents of the so-called "big history" model, which situates human history along a rather more expansive scale. Simply put, big history is a modern science-based creation story that starts with the Big Bang and ends with its entropic counterpart: the End of the Universe. One of its main proponents,

David Christian, explains in his magisterial work, *Maps of Time: An Introduction to Big History*, that even though there exist some fundamental similarities in the nature of all change in the universe, the task of the big history project is to explain how the rules of change vary at different scales. However, he also goes on to claim that: "Human history *is* different from cosmological history; but it is not *totally* different" (7). If evolution occurs across different scales and at different speeds—and if, on a human scale, we call it "culture" or "history", while on the scale of the geological epochs (e.g. the Pleistocene, the Holocene, the newly posited Anthropocene) we refer to it as "biology"—then the argument about the supposed purposefulness of its unfolding is not really sustainable, especially when we consider multiple evolutionary blind alleys and false starts.

The latter line of thinking has been developed most powerfully by the Polish author Stanisław Lem, who is best known to English readers as a science fiction writer but who also penned a number of philosophical commentaries on science, technology and evolution—the most accomplished of which is his 1964 treatise on futurology, technology, and science called *Summa Technologiae*. Serving as a perhaps unwitting counterpoint to the idealism that underpins Bergson's *Creative Evolution* with its notion of vital impetus (*élan vital*), Lem's *Summa* offers a much more sober, even ironic view of evolution, one that is rooted in the scientific method and in skepticism.[9] Lem's investigation into the parallel processes involved in biological and technical evolution, and his exploration of the

consequences of such parallelism, provide an important philosophical and empirical foundation for concepts that many humanities scholars use somewhat
loosely today, such as "life", "entanglement" and "relationality", while also stripping these concepts of any
vitalist hubris. For Lem, evolution "just happened",
we might say. This way of thinking is no doubt a blow
to anthropocentrism, which positions the human, and
human consciousness, as the pinnacle of all creation.
For Lem not only did evolution not have any "plan"
or "overarching idea" behind its actions, it also seems
to have moved in a series of jumps which were full of
mistakes, false starts, repetitions, and blind alleys. He
argues that any attempt to delineate a straight genea-
logical line of man would be completely futile, given
that attempts to descend to earth and walk on two feet
had been made by living beings over and over again
in the course of the evolutionary process. As Polish
critic and author of many publications on Lem, Jerzy
Jarzębski, points out, Lem also draws an important
distinction between biological evolution and the
evolution of reason, rejecting the assumption that an
increase in the latter automatically means improved
design capacity. Predating Richard Dawkins' idea of
evolution as a blind watchmaker by over two decades,
Lem's view of evolution is not just non-romantic; it is
also rather ironic—as manifested in the closing chapter of *Summa*, "A Lampoon of Evolution". Evolution
is described there as opportunistic, short-sighted,
miserly, extravagant, chaotic, and illogical in its design
solutions. Lem writes:

> We know very little about the way in which
> Evolution makes its "great discoveries", its
> revolutions. They do happen: they consist
> in creating new phyla. It goes without say-
> ing that also here evolution proceeds grad-
> ually—there is no other way. This is why
> we can accuse it of complete randomness.
> Phyla do not develop as a result of adapta-
> tions or carefully arranged changes but are
> a consequence of lots drawn in the evolu-
> tionary lottery—except very often, there is
> no top prize. (341)

The product of evolution that is of most interest to
us—i.e., the human—is seen by Lem as the last relic
of nature, which is itself in the process of being trans-
formed beyond recognition by the invasion of technology the human has introduced into his body and
environment. There is no mourning of this impending
change on Lem's part though, no attempt to defend
nature's ways and preserve the essential organic unity
of the human, since the latter is seen to be both transient and to some extent fictitious.

And yet, even though none of the entities in the
universe are indeed pre-planned or necessary, and
even though the human functions as a fictitious point
of unity in the non-purposeful unfolding of evolution,
one that in time will no doubt will be overcome by
other forms of matter's stabilization, the human's temporary presence in the duration of things poses him/
her with a unique responsibility. It is the nature of
this unique human responsibility within evolutionary

history that I am particularly interested in exploring in this book. Without rejecting this durational evolutionary framework of varying speeds, I therefore want to signal that we should perhaps remain cautious about presenting too neat an analogy between different temporalities and scales. However, rather than engage in ontological to-ing and fro-ing by trying to either defend an analogy or even contiguity, or postulate an inassimilable difference, between the two types of evolution, and, more broadly, between biology and culture, I want to suggest, yet again, that we turn instead to ethical questions that the debate opens before us. Indeed, the problem with the big history approach is not that it takes us beyond the realm of the human to look at larger scales but rather that that it naturalizes (in a straightforwardly humanist manner) the concept of complexity across cities and cells, with the technological events of human history perceived as planetary events without any deeper socio-political context or significance. Matter does not end up mattering here very much: its only orientation being its inscribed decay, which we as humans must do everything to prevent. Systemic equilibrium, understood in thermodynamic terms as energy conservation, is therefore the goal of the big historical project. "If Big Historians have a philosophy of media and technology, it is an entropic one. They share with politicians and industrialists the belief that what damns us may also save us and so negentropy comes to be figured as sustainability. In the wake of thermodynamics, sustainability has its own three laws: population control, climate change control and environmental equilibrium" (Kember and Zylinska XX). Postulating an "underlying unity" (Christian xxiv) of things, big history shores up the Anthropocene as a cross-scalar scarecrow figure, one that banishes the study of literature, art, sociology, politics, philosophy and economics to the dustbin of human history. The problem with big history is therefore first of all politico-ethical rather than ontological in that it puts forward a set of implicit technicist "fixes" to the Anthropocene, without reflecting on its own embeddedness in the network of human(ist) self-possession and self-interest. Taking seriously Rosi Braidotti's injunction to exercise "civic responsibility for the role of the academic today" (2013: 10), the chapters that follow will make more use of these old style "humanities" disciplines to come up with a better mode of thinking these political and ethical questions, thus hopefully contributing in a small way towards the development of a *post*-humanities framework.[10]

Notes

7. "There is nothing outside context" is another possible translation offered by Derrida to his famous statement, *il n'y a pas de hors-texte* (there is nothing outside the text), which some have mistakenly reduced to just saying that *language is all there is.*

8. Ingold argues that this "implied essentialisation of biology as a constant of human being, and of culture as its variable and interactive complement, is not just clumsily imprecise. It is the single major stumbling block that up to now has prevented us from moving

towards an understanding of our human selves, and of our place in the living world, that does not endlessly recycle the polarities, paradoxes and prejudices of western thought" (2004: 217).

9.   The material on Lem included in this and the next chapter has been partly reworked from the introduction I wrote to my translation of *Summa*, "Evolution May Be Greater Than the Sum of Its Parts, But It's Not All That Great: On Lem's *Summa Technnologiae*", which came out with the University of Minnesota Press in 2013.

10.   In her book *The Posthuman* Braidotti recognises the importance of defending the legacy of the humanities as an academic discipline, especially in the light of the critique this discipline is currently receiving in the neoliberal political regime. Her agenda for "post-human Humanities", premised on a radical reinvestment in critical thought and a creative engagement with technology, is outlined in the following terms: "The image of thought implied in the post-anthropocentric definition of the Human goes much further in the deconstruction of the subject, because it stresses radical relationality, that is to say non-unitary identities and multiple allegiances. As this shift occurs in a globalized and conflict-ridden world, it opens up new challenges in terms of both post-secular and post-nationalist perspectives [...] Against the prophets of doom, I want to argue that technologically mediated post-anthropocentrism can enlist the resources of bio-genetic codes, as well as telecommunication, new media and information technologies, to the task of renewing the Humanities. Posthuman subjectivity reshapes the identity of humanistic practices, by stressing heteronomy and multi-faceted relationality, instead of autonomy and self-referential disciplinary purity" (2013: 144-45).

Fig. 6: Joanna Zylinska, *Topia daedala* 6, 2014

Chapter 5

Humanity

This chapter provides some further historical and intellectual context for the concept of the human. This concept has not enjoyed a particularly good reception in recent critical theory: "the human" has been exposed by postructuralism and posthumanism as nothing more than a fantasy of unity and selfhood that excludes the human's dependency on other beings and non-living entities; it has been seen as too Eurocentric and masculinist by postcolonial and feminist theory; and has been revealed by various sciences to be just an arbitrary cut off point in the line of species continuity on the basis of characteristics shared across the species barrier: communication, emotions or tool use. Taking on board the critique coming from all these different quarters and its political and ethical force, I want to consider here the extent to which it is desirable or even possible to *return the human after the posthumanist critique.*[11] The reasons for this proposed return have nothing to do with any kind of residual humanism or species nostalgia. Instead, they spring from the recognition of the strategic role of the concept of the human in any kind of ethical project worth its salt, especially given that many of so-called posthumanist positions bring in humanism and other forms of essentialism through the back door of their theories anyway, under the guise of concepts such as love, kindness, relationality and co-emergence (see Zylinska 2012).

This (non- or post-humanist) human—one that could be written in quotation marks, placed under erasure, or, as I have done here, preceded by a qualifying adjective—entails the realization on the part of many theorists who still keep using this term that we are in (philosophical) trouble as soon as we start speaking about the human, but it also shows a certain intransigence that makes (some of) us hang on to the vestiges of the concept that has structured our thinking and philosophy for many centuries. There is no doubt something narcissistic about this enquiry into the instability of the human, inevitably conducted by a human subject, as is perhaps about the very practice of philosophy. But if narcissism is our way of relating, no matter if in a hospitable or violent way, to what we see as being different from us, then we should work towards what Derrida has called a "welcoming, hospitable narcissism, one that is much more open to the experience of the other as other" (1995: 199)—even if this other is already part of "us". The "we" of this sentence refers precisely to this critiqued, erased and qualified "human", but the latter needs to be seen as an ethical injunction directed at those of us who can get involved in the practices of thinking what it means to live a good life, in a professional or amateur capacity, rather than as any stable ontological designation. Instead, the human is positioned here a strategic designation that allows for the formulation and understanding of injunctions and ethical tasks of all kinds, one that remains aware of the history of philosophy and of its critique.

The plurality of this "human we" in the ethical context is not without problems: Emmanuel Levinas claims that ethical obligation *only ever applies to me*. For Levinas, "I am put in the passivity of an undeclinable assignation, in the accusative, a self. Not as a particular case of the universal, an ego belonging to the concept of ego, but as I, said in the first person— I, unique in my genus" (1998: 139). It is *my* anxiety about death and *my* awareness of my own mortality that place me on a linear and finite temporal scale while also creating a set of possibilities to be realized within that scale. These possibilities include the ultimate possibility of things coming to an end: they entail the end of me as a specimen of "humans" and the end of the human as a species. We may therefore go so far as to suggest that Levinas' ethics, which we will discuss in more detail later on, can be seen as a par excellence ethical framework for the Anthropocene because it makes me face up to the question of extinction across different scales. The humanism of Levinas' own ethics aside,[12] the perhaps unabashedly narcissistic singularity of the "I" of that framework itself poses us with a problem. This problem was poignantly captured by Timothy Morton, whose book of ecocriticism, *Ecology without Nature*, has been inspired to some extent by Levinas' notion of responsibility. Offering an account of his own writerly efforts to tell

a philosophical story of what counts as "Nature" and
how we humans perceive it differently, Morton writes:

> The more I try to evoke where I am—the
> "I" who is writing this text—the more
> phrases and figures of speech I must
> employ. I must get involved in a process
> of writing, the very writing that I am not
> describing when I evoke the environ-
> ment in which writing is taking place. The
> more convincingly I render my surround-
> ings, the more figurative language I end
> up with. The more I try to show you what
> lies beyond this page, the more of a page I
> have. And the more of a fictional "I" I have-
> splitting "me" into the one who is writing
> and the one who is being written about—
> the less convincing I sound. (2007: 30)

This kind of vacillation can perhaps be dismissed by
enemies of critical theory as philosophical navel-gaz-
ing, yet the suspension of human mastery—the mastery claimed both over himself and the universe—it
entails does provide a more viable grounding for an
ethical position that deems itself "minimal". It also
serves as a caution against any attempts to issue strong
ethical injunctions from this position, attempts that
seemingly forget about our human locatedness in evolution's "deep" history.

A more processual understanding of *evolution*—a
term Bergson uses interchangeably with notions such
as *movement* and *life*—will help us intuit that there is
no finality to evolutionary movement and, therefore,

that "the line of evolution that ends in man is not the only one" (Bergson xxii). Chemist Peter Butko points out that we humans "are not the crowning achievement of evolution, and it would indeed be strange if evolution stopped now" (102). However, even though we humans are just a temporary stabilization in the non-purposeful unfolding of the evolutionary process, our emergence in and with life arguably does pose us with a unique responsibility. This responsibility is partly historical, i.e., it is connected with our evolved ability to put our intuition and intellect to certain uses in order to reflect on what makes life good, and how to make life better—for ourselves and for others—while recognizing that there may exist an inherent antagonism between different entities and species in judging, or simply experiencing, such "goodness". Those others do not of course have to be human or even completely external to us: the universe itself is our most pressing "other". This is not to deny the fact that the key signal points of the human such as language, culture, tool use and emotions have actually been found across the species barrier.[13] Yet the historicity of this reflection on the human use of those products of evolution entails acknowledging that the *Homo sapiens* is also a *Homo faber moraliae*, that is that the human has developed a long tradition of reflecting on the emergence of customs, morals and values across culture—a practice to which s/he has given the name "ethics", and in which s/he has frequently resorted to storytelling. In other words, even if the difference between the human and other living entities is more of degree than of kind, to return to the Bergsonian terminology we have made use of before, ethics and storytelling are two sets of intertwined practices in which human singularity—which is not to be confused with human supremacy—has manifested itself in the Anthropocene (as well as the Holocene). They are also arguably tools through which the Anthropocene can be both apprehended and amended. The Anthropocene, as explained in the first chapter, names a new geological epoch that marks significant and irreversible human influence upon the geo- and biosphere via processes such as farming, deforestation, mining and urbanization. The term has been seen as controversial by many geologists; however, in this book it is used less as a scientific descriptor and more as an ethical pointer, outlining our human obligation towards the universe—of which we are only a tiny part.

An acknowledgement of the universal, "big-historical" scale across which things happen—something that does not come to us humans so easily and that is most often presented through a series of analogies—is a useful conceptual device for introducing humility into any ethical project that wants to make life in that tiny local irregularity of the universe called earth better. The minimalism of ethics thus proposed emerges as a result of the pragmatic recognition of the limitations of human faculties (reason *and* imagination, intellect *and* intuition). But it also becomes a meaningful injunction to pay attention to what "we humans"—who are temporary stabilizations of matter in that local irregularity of the universe called earth—are actually capable of grasping, from the midst of things, as it were. It is therefore an attempt to give an account of, and simultaneously counter, what astrophysicists call "the strong anthropic principle", a tendency to explain the universe from our human standpoint, as if it existed uniquely *for us humans*. As Hawking clarifies,

> We have developed from the geocentric cosmologies of Ptolemy and his forebears, through the heliocentric cosmology of Copernicus and Galileo, to the modern picture in which the earth is a medium-sized planet orbiting around an average star in the outer suburbs of an ordinary spiral galaxy, which is itself only one of about a million million galaxies in the observable universe. Yet the strong anthropic principle would claim that this whole vast construction simply exists for our sake. This is very hard to believe. Our Solar System is certainly a prerequisite for our existence, and one might extend this to the whole of our galaxy to allow for an earlier generation of stars that created the heavier elements. But there does not seen to be any need for all those other galaxies, nor for the universe to be so uniform in every direction on the large scale. (126)

The recognition of this non-necessity of the universe, and of the emergence of life—including conscious life—in it, does not diminish our responsibility for this medium-sized planet we call home and its surroundings, or for its human and nonhuman inhabitants. However, it does potentially strip any mode of philosophizing about it off a certain explanatory and interventionist hubris. This kind of posthumanist, or better, non-anthropocentric standpoint poses a challenge to human exceptionalism, but it also remains accountable, to cite Barad, "for the role we play in the differential constitution and differential positioning of the human among other creatures (both living and nonliving)" (136). So even though *it is not all about us*, we humans have a singular responsibility to give an account of the differentiations of matter, of which we are part. Ethics is therefore constitutively linked with poetics, because it comes to us through stories, i.e. through narratives of different genres and kinds. It is through the latter that we make sense of the world and pass on instructions on how to live to younger generations. We need such instructions because we come into the world unformed, lacking the basic capacities to move within it, communicate with others and transform our surroundings. In other words, we lack *sophia*, widely conceived wisdom, which stands for both intelligence and affective-motoric know-how, and without which we are equally inclined to create and destroy ourselves and others, to make love and war (see Stiegler). It is only though relationality with what is not in us—with other living beings but also with the widely conceived "environment" that consists of animate and inanimate entities and processes—that we can activate the life that moves us, and it is only through instruction in wisdom that we can learn to apprehend our own situatedness in the network of ever changing relations.

From our own narrow and earth-bound human point of view, there is something rather tragic about the universe and the way it unfolds in such a seemingly futile manner. Our attempts to construct civilizations, philosophies and religions are ways of overcoming this futility, even if the very notion of futility is itself a product of those civilizations, philosophies and religions. Anthropocentrism becomes our shield in this struggle, one that has served us well through centuries but that we may want to put down if we want to avoid being like a child who thinks he has become invisible only because he has closed his eyes. With our eyes closed, we will not be able to see the evolutionary unfolding which is likely to sweep us away at some point (although there may be reasons why we may prefer to miss out on this particular event). This anthropocentric shield will also hide from us the unfolding of the technoevolutionary process which we ourselves put in motion and which is still reversible, at least theoretically. Yet Stanisław Lem, whose aforementioned 1964 book *Summa Technologiae* is one of the most powerful accounts of evolution and the human's place in it, has serious doubts about the likelihood of any such reversal on our part. Moving beyond the anthropocentric framework in which the human is seen as occupying the very top of the chain of beings, Lem nevertheless spends a good deal of time considering humans' singularity in the cosmic universe, as well as their moral and political responsibility. The Polish author remains skeptical with regard to the rationality of human beings. As Lem puts it rather ominously, "Man knows more about his dangerous tendencies than he did a hundred years ago, and in the next hundred years his knowledge will be even more advanced. Then he will make use of it" (2013: 6). It becomes quite clear that Lem is not very optimistic about the human as the product of evolution—not just in terms of our future developmental prospects, as mentioned above, but also in terms of our current ethico-political situation. This is perhaps unsurprising since, as explained in the previous chapter, evolution cannot be trusted with knowing what it is doing. Neither, seemingly, can we—at least not always or consistently—because we lack wisdom that would prevent us from entering into unnecessary conflict. This limitation results from an underlying conflict "between a conscious mind that can think and an underlying program that determines action", i.e., genes, as explained by N. Katherine Hayles (29).

What is the human to do in the light of this conflict? According to Lem, "the traditionally inherited types of ethics are all rapidly becoming impotent" (Swirski 115). Living through the collapse of various forms of authority, secularization, the emergence of both extreme nationalisms and extreme regionalisms, as well as the pathologies of escapism, the modern human faces a kind of *horror vacui*, "giving us as a result a new type of 'man without conscience'" (Swirski 114). Such pessimism and sorrow about the human condition is obviously a familiar trope in both philosophy and literature. Yet we have to distinguish here between the pessimistic view of the human as encapsulated by many metaphysical narratives, including those of the dominant religions, whereby man is suffering from some kind of original sin or some other innate fault that predisposes him to doing evil, and the more skeptical-realist argument, which evaluates human faults empirically, so to speak, on the basis of historical experience. Furthermore, this positing of the potential to do evil is an argument through subtraction: the human will eventually make use of the acquired knowledge and put it to various uses, including harmful ones, because there is nothing inherent either in the human or the world to stop this course of action. (Pseudo-scientific theories of evolutionary ethics, whereby our moral intuitions are seen as evolved forms of behavior that protect us against our genes and the supposed "truth" they carry, fall apart both against circumstantial evidence and rigorous philosophical enquiry into their founding assumptions.)

Political systems, state and organizational policies, moral codes, and cultural values may serve as barriers against such negative and damaging turns of events. However, in most cases politics and ethics find it difficult to catch up with the development of science. As a consequence they arrive too late to prevent various events from happening. This restricted freedom with regard to his/her own agency, combined with the lack of knowledge about being with others in the world, contribute to the human's self-diagnosed tragic condition discussed earlier. Lem is less inclined to offer solutions to this state of events, even if he does recognize the role of ethics as a structural device used to contain human aggression and violence. Betrization, a procedure from his novel *Return from the Stars* which is executed upon all human fetuses in order to tame their violent impulses, is raised as an ironic proposition, with the belief that any solution to the human "evil" would have to be technicist. (Incidentally, a similar argument returns, less ironically, in Emmott's book, *Ten Billion*—and is actually already applied by the pharmaceutical industry in the so-called developed world through the widespread propagation of antidepressants and ADHD medication.)

Drawing on this line of thought that sees ethics as a uniquely human intervention into the world which is quintessentially nonhuman, the minimal ethics outlined throughout this book tries to move beyond the lethargy of irony and the instrumentalism of technical fixes. Minimal ethics is therefore less a solution and more a proposition—*a proposition to put up the question of ethics on the current agenda*, alongside other, seemingly more pressing and global issues such sustainability, climate change, fossil fuel crisis, human survival, etc. Unless we are prepared to do this, and to position ethics itself as a particularly pressing issue for the Anthropocene, we run the danger of falling prey either to anthropocentric moralism (where values are being laid out without questioning the process of their fabrication and the conflict in which they always exist with some other values) or to delegating authority to technology which remains underpinned by instrumentalist assumptions. It goes without saying that any form of ethics thus posited needs to remain technically aware—i.e., it needs to take responsibility for our technical genealogy and technical future, to manage technology while seeing ourselves and the world

in and with which we emerge as inherently technical—instead of being positioned as a human weapon
against technology. Indeed, ethics itself is always a
form of technics, a reaching out beyond the confines of the human(ist) moral self to other forms of
becoming in the universe, many of which the human
is coevolving with. However, even though the ethical
human subject is to be seen as relational, and hence
technological and prosthetic, this does not mean that
any interventions to his biogenetic make-up, or to the
make-up of his environment, will have to be seen as
morally equal. The minimal ethical task that emerges
here consists in knowing how to differentiate between
different forms of relationality, or, in other words, how
to manage technics well, as much as we can, in the little time that we have left.

One final issue that needs addressing here is that
of the ontological and ethical status of "animals" in
this framework—a term I have so far eschewed using
in this book. Even though I recognize the important
political work undertaken both by animal studies
scholars and animal activists in drawing attention to
animal suffering or even managing to reduce it, I am
also aware of the limitations of this all-encompassing
concept, embracing both pets and pests; companion
species with a recognizable "face" as well as spiders,
seahorses, sloths and shrews. The problem is not
fully resolved by incorporating the human into the
wider specter of animality because the actual gesture
of obviating "the human-animal distinction" can only
ever be made from the point of species difference (see
Zylinska 2012)—although such an argument can be

useful in challenging human superiority and special positioning across evolutionary unfoldings. Yet in any such attempts the human *desire to philosophize about the animal* (or even about himself *as animal*) remains surprisingly free from critical enquiry: many scholars seem oblivious of the fact that any suspension or abandonment of the human-animal distinction, just like any form of thinking about the animal as the human's supposed "other", can only be undertaken from within the anthropocentric position of cognitive superiority, with all the hegemonic authority it entails and confirms. The strategic use of the term "human" in this book is therefore not coupled with an equally strategic embracing of its "animal" equivalent, precisely because the latter is not its equivalent. The typological gap we are introducing here should be seen as first and foremost an ethical orientation rather than as an absolute epistemological or ontological differentiation. Morton's term "strange strangers" (2010: 41) can help us in designating this orientation, without reintroducing any radical differences between species or life forms, because all these "strange strangers" are mutually enmeshed. However, ethics is not a mutuality: as explained before, the responsibility that arises here is not so much just even human but only ever *mine*. The "I" here does not stand for a Kantian individual self-present moral subject, but rather for an entangled and dynamically constituted node in the network of relations to whom an address is being made and upon whom an obligation is being placed, and who is thus made-temporarily-singular precisely via this address.

Notes

11. This chapter develops further some of the ideas raised in my article, "Bioethics Otherwise, or, How to Live with Machines, Humans, and Other Animals".

12. I discuss the humanist limitations of Levinas' ethics in my *Bioethics in the Age of New Media*, while also providing a justification for salvaging the notion of ethical responsibility from Levinas' work for a non-anthropocentric ethical theory. I return to this latter point in various sections of this book.

13. For a discussion of how the behaviors that used to be seen as uniquely human have now been found across the species barrier, see Zylinska, "Bioethics Otherwise, or, How to Live with Machines, Humans, and Other Animals".

Fig. 7: Joanna Zylinska, *Topia daedala* 7, 2014

Chapter 6

Ontology

"The world" does not really name any kind of objective external reality. Rather, as I suggested in chapter two, this term should be understood as first and foremost referring to a temporary mental organization, undertaken by a spatially embedded and embodied human, of the various processes of which she is part. To say this is by no means to deny the existence of things beyond our representation or imagining of it; it is just to acknowledge the limitations of our cognition and language in grasping things *as they* (supposedly) *are*. Imposing unity on them through the concept of "the world" (or, equally, separating them with our intellect into those very "things") is therefore nothing more than a mental operation, an operation which is conditioned by our adopted theoretical and linguistic frameworks. This kind of mental operation becomes a way of domesticating the enormity and complexity of our universe, as is made evident in Neil Shubin's popular science book, *The Universe Within*. Citing the American philosopher William James, Shubin says that religious experience is said to emanate precisely "from 'feeling at home in the universe'", which is similar to how Kant explained the mechanism of the sublime, with our mind ultimately triumphant over the failure of our imagination to grasp extreme scales or complex dynamics precisely because it can theorize this failure, and thus obtain consolation. For scientist Shubin consolation comes from our acknowledgement of the unity of cosmic matter across different scales in the universe, even if we cannot see or fully grasp those scales. He writes: "With bodies composed of particles derived from the birth of stellar bodies and containing organs shaped by the workings of planets, eroding rock, and the action of the seas, it is hard not to see home everywhere" (185).

Consolation and cosmic domesticity are desired by us humans precisely because the majority of processes in the so-called "world" (or, indeed, "universe") across its different scales unfold outside and beneath both human agency and human consciousness, in ways that we can at best describe with mathematical equations but that we cannot ever obtain a "total" picture of. Some think it is just a matter of developing better physics or better telescopes. However, I am in agreement with the proponents of flat ontology such as Bruno Latour, Graham Harman and Levi R. Bryant, who claim that "the world does not exist"—*even if myself I retain the need to use the term strategically*. Yet, even while doing this, I follow Bryant in asserting that "there is no 'super-object', Whole, or totality that would gather all objects together in a harmonious unity" (32). This, I should signal, is perhaps my only substantial point of agreement with object-oriented philosophy, a recently popular framework of thought which debunks traditional ("correlationist") philosophy as humanist while at the same time occluding its own foundational, and not any less humanist, gesture. Indeed, object-oriented philosophy's ontological ambitions are premised on the very correlationist principles its authors critique in proponents of other modes of philosophizing about "the world".

It is this unexamined desire to construct ontologies, be it flat or layered ones, that is most troubling for me in the work of many contemporary thinkers today—including a number of process philosophers, who seem not to attend to the processuality of the process all that carefully. Indeed, for many, "process" becomes just a tool in the building of worlds, even if the actual worlds produced are deemed unstable, open, fluid. More often than not, such worlds are just gifts that the (usually male) philosopher charms out of his hat and passes on to his followers. To put it bluntly—although I aim to defend this statement later on—this intellectual trend towards ontology-building is not just masculinist but also, in a bizarrely achronological way, pre-feminist. Many of the thinkers I am hinting at here—not just the object-oriented ontology "school" but also political philosophers of the more continental bent such as Alain Badiou or Slavoj Žižek—defend the ontological modes of the thinking they promote through the supposed urgency of the current political conjuncture, offering various forms of critique of the emasculation of philosophy by sophistry and calling for a return to philosophy "proper" (see Braidotti 2013: 5).[14] Badiou deserves a special mention here as a self-fashioned lone voice in a philosophical desert, a defender of ontology and

the truth process amidst the cacophony of deception
and rhetorical half-truths. This is why I want to spend
some time looking at the ontological desire espoused
yet also partly occluded in his work—especially as I
aim to position *minimal* ethics as a viable way to continue philosophizing in a counter-ontological, post-
masculinist way.

Significantly, it is common-or-garden ethics that
evokes Badiou's particular ire. In the Introduction to
Ethics, a little book originally intended for sixth-form-
ers, he writes:

> Certain scholarly words, after long con-
> finement in dictionaries and in academic
> prose, have the good fortune, or the mis-
> fortune—a little like an old maid who,
> long since resigned to her fate, suddenly
> becomes, without understanding why, the
> toast of the town—of sudden exposure to
> the bright of day, of being plebi- and publi-
> cited, press-released, televised, even men-
> tioned in government speeches. The word
> *ethics*, which smacks so strongly of phi-
> losophy courses and its Greek root, which
> evokes Aristotle (*The Nicomachean Ethics*,
> one of the great bestsellers!), has today
> taken centre stage. (2001: 1)

The traditional kind of ethics that Badiou critiques,
and that his own book *Ethics* is written against, is
compared here to a woman—"an old maid", not
very attractive and yet clearly gagging for it, without
much hope that it's actually going to happen—who

suddenly becomes the toast of the town. Everyone suddenly wants to have a bit of her, to have a share of her old maidenhood. Traditional ethics, the ethics of evil, of victimhood and of morals, might be a little "minging", it's a potential little slapper resigned to her solitude only to find herself suddenly on the stage, pole-dancing before the audience of randy, red-faced punters. Against this somewhat distasteful image of ethics as an old maid freely dispensing her not-so-attractive gifts, an ethics which "smacks so strongly of philosophy courses" but which in fact only masquerades as true philosophy, Badiou sets his ethics of truths: rigid, focused and solemn. It is an ethics that Peter Hallward calls "decisive" and Simon Critchley describes as "heroic". The gaping hole of the slapper can be opposed here with the composure of an ascetic whose motto is "Keep going" (aka the Badiouan-Lacanian "*Continuez*").

Badiou's critique applies in particular to the ethics of sympathy for the other, a mode of thinking which only in fact keeps the other in his or her place, and which, under the guise of the celebration of difference, confines this other to the oppressive category of the "victim" while simultaneously constructing a hierarchy of bigger and lesser forms of oppression. His book *Ethics* is an attack on "a generalised victimization" inherent in the ideology of human rights and a defense of the antihumanism of the 1960s. According to Badiou, Western hegemonic politics (what he calls "democratic totalitarianism", 2001: lv) legitimizes its actions (e.g. intervention in Serbia, in Afghanistan) through moralizing sermons. Even though I am

advocating ethics as a "better" mode of philosophizing than ontology, I do share Badiou's concerns
regarding replacing politics with the "mindless cat-
echism" (2001: liii) or "moral terrorism" of contemporary culturalist ethical discourses, which in fact
serve Western capitalism and its many institutions,
where "goodness" itself becomes a good to be traded
in. The multiplicity of "the world" becomes reduced
to the knowable sequence of important human (and
increasingly nonhuman) others, such as "animals",
with their particularist struggles being prioritized in
terms of bigger and lesser oppression. As a result of
this way of thinking, politics becomes subordinated to
ethics, to the single perspective that really matters in
this conception of things: the sympathetic and indig-
nant judgment of the spectator of the circumstances
(2001: 9). This type of ethics, according to Badiou,
results in "the unrestrained pursuit of self-interest, the
disappearance or extreme fragility of emancipatory
politics, the multiplication of 'ethnic' conflict, and
the universality of unbridled competition" (10). The
human being is defined here as a victim, as "the being
who is capable of recognizing himself as a victim"
(10). This notion of ethics, argues Badiou, "prohib-
its every broad, positive vision of possibilities" (14);
ethics becomes only a "conservation by the so-called
'West' of what it possesses" (14).

However, it should perhaps be clarified here that
this girly, weepy thing that Badiou condemns as ethics
is really an old-fashioned moralism, which, in Wendy
Brown's words, stands for "a reproachful moralizing
sensibility", "or a kind of posture or pose taken up in

the ruins of morality by its faithful adherents" (2001: 22-23). Although morality as well as moralism arise out of the subject's unacknowledged attachment to a given idea of truth, and to identity positioned in terms of injury, moralism is particularly harmful, as it replaces the passion of a quasi-religious conviction which is nevertheless capable of inspiring an emancipatory movement with paranoia, mania and, ultimately, political stasis (see Zylinska 2009: 153). In the light of this dismissal of ethics, Badiou wheels out his ontological weapons: singular truths are the only thing that can provide a grounding for a viable ethical framework for him, a proposition that is markedly different from the various forms of the ethics of alterity (Levinas, Irigaray), antagonism (Mouffe, Butler) or relationality (Braidotti) that have been prevalent in cultural theory over the recent decades.

Indeed, Badiou insists that his "ethics of truths" must remain a-relational and hence a-social because it compels distance from commonplace opinion, introducing a clash between post-evental fidelity and "the normal pace of things" (2001: 54). A rhythmic vacillation is clearly implied here: it springs from the disturbance of the regular order by the irruption of the extraordinary. This is the moment in which we are endowed with a task of having to remain faithful to this *event* (or, rather, to our naming of it), i.e. having to live the consequences of its nomination. Badiou writes, "An evental fidelity is a real break [...] in the specific order within which the event took place" (42). A truth is thus always post-evental; it is a name which is extracted from the void (see Badiou 1991).

Another way of understanding the event—one of the key terms in Badiou's philosophy—is as an eruption of the novelty that obliges one to think the situation, or as a provisional suspension of the multiplicity of interpretations (which implies a prior recognition of this multiplicity). The event is thus a breach of the ordinary by the extraordinary, an exposure and explosion of our animality by something that has happened and that makes us "decide a *new* way of being" (Badiou 2001: 41).

The imagery of seizure and interruption, of puncturing and piercing through, is recurrent in Badiou's writings. A truth process enabled by the event "punches a hole" in our knowledges of the situation (43) and prompts us to think again, anew. I am "seized by the not-known", and, "as a result [of the event], I am also suspended, broken, annulled; disinterested" (49-51). "[T]he piercing-through of an encounter" composes a subject (52), while "[e]ach faithful truth-process is an entirely immanent break with the situation" (44). Yet it is difficult for me to pass without comment over this sense of seizure and piercing through, of uprightness and rigidity, of violence and irruption, of Badiou's philosophy, and the language through which it is conveyed. I am aware that Badiou himself not only shows little interest in linguistic games but is in fact actively committed to "freeing philosophy from the tyranny of language". Those who are preoccupied with linguistic interpretation and language games, supporters of what Badiou, after Lyotard, calls "The Great Linguistic Turn" of Western Philosophy (1999: 94), are deemed sophists, and thus positioned as anti-philosophers, who are nevertheless "useful" in marking the beginning of a new philosophical era which Badiou is hoping to inaugurate. Badiou writes, "The sophist is from the outset the enemy-brother, philosophy's implacable twin" (1999: 116). The trouble is that contemporary sophists frequently masquerade as "great philosophers", playing with their veils and mirrors to create an illusion that "the fundamental opposition is not between truth and error or wandering, but between speech and silence, between what can be said and what is impossible to say" (116-17). Denying the existence of truth, the sophist's claims only support convention, rules and language games—where the seriousness of truth as the central category of philosophy is required, the sophist, "a perverted double of the philosopher" (133), is only interested in playing (or, perhaps even, in playing with himself). But philosophy's task is by no means to annihilate the sophist—as Badiou puts it, "No, the sophist must only be assigned to his place" (133). The sophist's unruliness, his constant stepping out of line, his shadowing of the philosophy with his illusions and performances, his conniving tricks, have to be terminated, if the return of and to philosophy is to be accomplished.

The actual "sophists" referred to in Badiou's writings are predominantly male philosophers (Nietzsche, Wittgenstein, Derrida, to name but a few). But let us ponder for a moment whether it is not the *femininity* of the sophist, i.e., his position as a woman, a figure of masquerade, pretense and non-truth, that needs to be expelled from philosophy for it to continue in its

systemic (rigid, correct and erect) manner. Derrida's
Spurs offers a mocking explication of precisely such
a masquerade in which woman as the "truth of non-
truth" deceives and disguises the truth of philosophy
with her artful tricks:

> Since [woman] is a model for truth she
> is able to display the gifts of her seduc-
> tive power, which rules over dogmatism,
> and disorients and routs those credulous
> men, the philosophers. And because she
> does not believe in the truth (still, she
> does find that uninteresting truth in her
> interest) woman remains a model, only
> this time a good model. But because she
> is a good model she is in fact a bad model.
> She plays at dissimulation, at ornamenta-
> tion, deceit, artifice, at an artist's philoso-
> phy. (1979: 67)

From the vantage point of "philosophy proper", the
minimal ethics outlined throughout this volume
would be seen as precisely such a masquerade, an
exercise in sophistry that does not offer any truths,
engaging instead in the game of smoke and mirrors.
Admittedly, its twenty one theses outlined in the
Conclusion perhaps read more like poetry. And yet in
its withholding of truths and its lack of desire to build
"worlds" and pass them off as reality, it is premised
on one strong injunction directed at the human who
is already involved in the game of philosophizing—
either professionally, as a scholar, writer or theolo-
gian, or, in a broader sense, as someone trying to make

sense of how to live a good life: *an injunction to keep a check on one's ontologizing ambitions.* To recognize the human activity of sense-making and the human orientation towards what is not in her already entails an ethical challenge: to respond to the difference of what we are calling "the world".

"Difference" is not of course a problem-free category—Badiou points out that "There are as many differences, say, between a Chinese peasant and a young Norwegian professional as between myself and anybody at all, including myself". (And then he adds, "As many, but also, then, neither more nor less" (2001: 26).) What Badiou seems to be doing here is emptying the philosophy of difference of its meaningfulness, i.e., reducing it to the absurd, to banality, to vacuity. As it is such an obvious and commonplace thing to notice that people are different from each other, it is really a waste of time (and of political energy) to go on about these differences—it is boring, facile and counter-productive. Yet the notion of difference within the minimal ethics outlined here is also, we might say … minimal. It refers to the ongoing process of differentiation that is immanent to matter, and hence to what we are calling "the world", and that mainly occurs outside and beyond the human—but it still calls upon the human to take responsibility for the differentiating cuts into the flow of life s/he is herself making with his/her tongue, language, or tools. Minimal ethics for the Anthropocene is therefore less about building a better world as an external unity and more about making better cuts into that which we are naming the world. But, to avoid becoming yet another masculinist enterprise which knows in advance and once and for all what it is striving for, the minimal ethics proposed here has to embrace the very openness and vagueness of its premises. It needs to recognize in itself the indecency, the gaudiness, the masquerade of any attempt to make philosophy, and then to try and make it better—which perhaps means smaller, less posturing, less erect.

Notes

14. In *The Posthuman* Braidotti interprets this state of events as indicative of a broader move away from various forms of more speculative critical theory in the early twenty-first century humanities: "It is as if, after the great explosion of theoretical creativity of the 1970s and 1980s, we had entered a zombified landscape of repetition without difference and lingering melancholia. A spectral dimension has seeped into our patterns of thinking, boosted, on the right of the political spectrum, by ideas about the end of ideological time (Fukuyama, 1989) and the inevitability of civilizational crusades (Huntington, 1996). On the political left, on the other hand, the rejection of theory has resulted in a wave of resentment and negative thought against the previous intellectual generations. In this context of theory-fatigue, neo-communist intellectuals (Badiou and Žižek, 2009) have argued for the need to return to concrete political action, even violent antagonism if necessary, rather than indulge in more theoretical speculations. They have contributed to push the philosophical theories of post-structuralism out of fashion" (5).

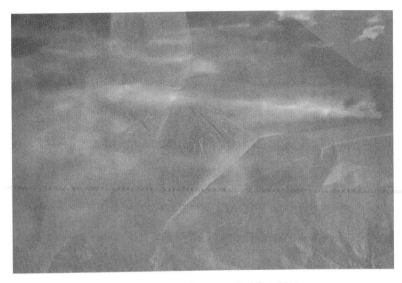

Fig. 8: Joanna Zylinska, *Topia daedala* 8, 2014

Chapter 7

Ethics

Ethics is a mode of human locatedness in the world which involves a recognition of the processual and unstable nature not only of any such locatedness but also of the human that is thus located. It also involves the human in giving an account of the modes of relationality that ensue. In this sense, ethics is not just about being-in but also about being-with. The processual and co-emergent nature of what we are calling the world applies to all sorts of thickenings of matter across different scales, as argued earlier. All beings in the world exist and emerge "with". Humans are not the only beings that are capable of relating to and collaborating with others; they are also most probably not the only sentient beings that are capable of communicating with others, grasping others' pain, causing violence to others but also withholding or at least minimizing violence. It is quite likely that what we conventionally refer to as moral behavior—actions that are compliant with a given group's customs and social codes and that are aimed to produce beneficial outcomes for this group, on a material or spiritual level—is just a set of reactions to external and internal stimuli,[15] reactions that then become a form of learned behavior and that, in the human language, get elevated to the status of "goodness". It is primarily the linguistic labelling of certain types of behavior as "good", "noble" and "honorable" that differentiates human acts towards other human and nonhuman entities and processes as "moral". As a consequence, beings that humans designate as "animals" are always kept on the other side of morality, in a denigrated position described as "animality".[16] As John Mullarkey points out, "members of one group, *Homo sapiens*, have distributed among themselves every right and privilege through the course of an enlarging enfranchisement". They have achieved this state of events by "invoking an identity that necessarily ostracises a vast out-group ('non-human animals' so called) to the extent of either defining them in some jurisdictions as non-sentient beings or practically treating them as such in most others" (97).

The point of the argument presented thus far is not to expand the notion of ethics to other sentient beings beyond the human. Indeed, such conceptual "expansionism" only ends up confirming the singular human moral subject, with other beings (dolphins, apes) assessed on the basis of how closely they replicate human behavior and thus how closely they approach the human's "humanity".[17] Instead, I propose to see ethics as a relatively narrow cultural practice, worked out by humans across history, as a form of regulating ways of co-existing and co-emerging with others. This cultural practice also involves providing an account— verbally, experientially, or aesthetically—of these processes of co-existence and co-emergence. In others words, ethics could be described as a practice of not only becoming in and with the world but also of working out possibilities for what we will decide, through deliberation, policy work and conflict resolution, to be ways of *becoming better* in the world. Once again, this is not to deny that so-called animals are incapable of enacting conventionally understood moral behavior such as empathy, cooperation, fairness or reciprocity, or that they may even turn out to be more successful than humans at displaying such behavior. It is just to propose to reserve the term "ethics" to that narrow spectrum of humans' affective-cognitive responses and actions that involve giving an account of these behaviors, via the conventionally (even if not *exclusively*) human cultural practices such as philosophy, story-telling and art. Put yet otherwise, ethics is a historically contingent human mode of becoming in the world, of becoming different from the world, and of narrating and taking responsibility for the nature of this difference. There are no prior limits to the applicability of this ethics, which is why we could say that it involves accounting for something as wide and abstract as "our place in the sun" (Levinas 1989: 82-5). This account is necessary because any place in the universe I temporally occupy, and from which I build, consume, love and destroy, is never originally and duly mine: I am just a wayfarer through matter's planetary unfoldings and thickenings. There is therefore a story-telling aspect to ethics.

The defense of ethics as a "better" mode of philosophizing, one that precedes ontology and that makes a demand on being, comes from the thought of Emmanuel Levinas. This precedence takes place on the level of justice: if ontology is a "philosophy of power" that reduces any ideas about what we are calling the world and its unfolding to the conceptual apparatus possessed by the cognizant subject (Levinas 1969: 46), ethics can be seen instead as the suspension of humans' epistemological and hence domineering pretensions. This is not to say that we humans have to remain ignorant; it is just to suggest caution in getting to know things all too quickly and then constantly producing and reproducing behavior and action, or ethics and politics, on the basis of this knowledge. Turning to Levinas in any work that aims to promote post-anthropocentric thinking the way this book does is of course not without problems, given the significant role ascribed to the human face as the source of ethical demand in his writings, and the marked (even if historically comprehensible, given the context of the Shoah) disinterestedness in other nonhuman forms of being and becoming. However, I argued elsewhere that Levinas' "error" is first of all scientific and historical rather than philosophical, in that he does not consider seriously the limitations of his own concept of the human as a speaking being with the face, rather than a sentient being reaching to—and touched by—others in a myriad different ways (see Zylinska 2009: 57). Yet do we really know with whom we can enter into a discourse (a refugee? a dolphin? a computer bot?) and what this "entering into a discourse" actually means? Levinas' ethics also does not go all the way in recognizing the mutual entanglement of "us" and "the world": the boundaries of Levinas' "other", even if not fully knowable, are nevertheless transcendentally posited, rather than seen as immanent, as differentiation-from-within—which is the line of thought adopted in this book.

The minimal ethics for the Anthropocene is therefore not Levinasian in any obvious sense but it does borrow its minimalist structuring from his rethinking of the edifice of Western philosophy, and especially of the relationship between ethics and politics. It also borrows from Levinas the sense of ethical obligation and responsibility as something inevitable that makes a demand on the human and that demands a response from him/her. It becomes, to cite Timothy Morton, a form of "radical openness to everything" (2010: 15). This openness in itself does not guarantee the taking up of the ethical challenge by the thus interpellated human but it does position her as always already involved, obligated, entangled. In a counterargument to neo-Darwinian theories of the selfish gene, Morton playfully argues that it is altruism rather than selfishness that can be said to be hardwired into reality, since "we are made of others: we've literally got them under our skin" (119). Indeed, Lynn Margulis' research into evolutionary biology (1998) has conclusively shown that, thanks to the age-old processes of genetic symbiosis we carry within ourselves traces of our microbial ancestors. Rather than being seen as Dawkins' teleological "lumbering robots" equipped with the task of transmitting and hence preserving DNA for future generations of living beings, humans are posited here as always nomadic, as transient and temporary stabilizations of life whose form emerges in relation with their environment. To use Bergson's poetic language,

> life is like a current passing from germ to germ through the medium of a developed organism. It is as if the organism itself were only an excrescence, a bud caused to sprout by the former germ endeavoring to continue itself in a new germ. The essential thing is the continuous progress indefinitely pursued, an invisible progress, on which each visible organism rides during the short interval of time given it to live. (1944: 32).

From this vantage point, humans do not have any pre-designed tasks, even at genetic level: they are just temporarily stabilized processes that are as accidental as any others, and shorter-lived than most at that.

It is through Bergson's attention to life—as outlined in his *Creative Evolution* but formulated in more clearly ethical terms in *The Two Sources of Morality and Religion*, that I aim to draw on Levinas' ethical intimations. Mullarkey justifies such a philosophical encounter by arguing that "Bergsonism may best be read as an ethics of alterity fleshed out in empirical concerns" (107) but also that Levinas' idea of relationality *qua* responsibility which is foundational to ethics has been influenced by Bergson. Indeed, Mullarkey goes so far as to suggest that "*élan vital* itself is but another way of thinking about alterity", with Bergson's absolutely new becoming the Levinasian

"Other" (109).[18] If life itself amounts to the creation of forms ever new, the nature of social relations is also "an ongoing creation" (Mullarkey 1999: 88)—a line of argument that returns in the work of many contemporary thinkers of entanglement such as Haraway, Barad or Braidotti. With this perspective, as Mullarkey explains, "Bergson sidesteps the frozen essentialism of reductive naturalists as well as the liquid relativism of culturalists: society is indeed moulded by nature, but by a creative nature which in part tries to break its own moulds!" (89).

The fact that we humans have literally got others under our skin does not yet make us unique amongst other beings, but the historical practice of reflecting on such forms of relationality with others, via philosophy, story-telling and art, does. What is unique on the social level is therefore not the nature of these relations as such—indeed, they are part of the wider evolution of life—but rather the human possibility of taking (at least partial) responsibility for some of those relations, and giving (an equally partial) account of them. Our human responsibility can therefore be described as a form of experiential, corporeal and affective "worlding" in which we produce (knowledge about) the world, seen as a set of relations and tasks. This may involve relating responsibly to other humans, but also to nonhuman beings and processes, including some extremely tiny and extremely complex or even abstract ones (microbes, clouds, climate, global warming). Taking responsibility for something we cannot see is not easy. But, as Morton, argues, "it's no tougher than taking responsibility for, say, not killing—you don't have to come up with a reason; you just do it and figure out why later. That's why it's called an ethical decision. It doesn't have to be proved or justified. You just do it." This is not an advocacy of an "anything goes" form of ethics; only a recognition that "one can act spontaneously *and* consciously" (2010: 99, emphasis added). Our response is thus a way of taking responsibility for the multiplicity of the world, and for our relations to and with it. Such responsibility can always be denied or withdrawn, but a response will have already taken place nonetheless. However, an act of taking responsibility is not just a passive reaction to pre-existing reality: it involves actively making cuts into the ongoing unfolding of matter in order to stabilize it. Ethical de-cisions can thus be best understood as material in-cisions.

The language of incisions and cuts highlights an important aspect of the ethics outlined here: the inevitability of violence as its constitutive element, rather than as something that should be expunged and overcome the way Morton seems to suggest (2010: 127-8). For me, dependency and violence are inevitable conditions of relationality and "worlding". Given that the latter involves the voluntary and involuntary shaping of matter across the geo- and biosphere, it may incur changing its temporary stabilizations, destroying things, causing pain to sentient beings or even killing them. Of course, such practices "should never leave their practitioners in moral comfort, sure of their righteousness", as Donna Haraway poignantly emphasizes (2003: 75). The recognition of the inevitability of violence in any relation does not take away the injunction to both minimize the violence and reflect on it. In other words, it involves working towards what Levinas termed "good violence" (1969): a rupture within the self which is made to face the difference and relate to it. There is no mutuality here: as mentioned before, this ethical responsibility is only ever not so much even human as it is *mine*. It is therefore singular, singularly allocated and enacted. Yet the subject of this ethics has nothing to do with the individualism and self-possession of normative moral theories: instead, it is decisively posthuman. Such a subject can be defined, after Braidotti, as relational, "constituted in and by multiplicity"; it is a subject "that works across differences and is also internally differentiated, but still grounded and accountable" (2013: 49). An ethical theory that embeds violence into its framework—rather than just sweeping it aside in a fantasy gesture of moral purification—promises to address the question of co-emergence and co-dependency in all its complexity. This does not imply imposing moral equivalence between all forms of violence and all forms of dependency, even if we accept that "[a]ny act of identification, naming, or relation is a betrayal of and a violence toward the Other" (Calarco 2008: 136).

Injunctions with regard to what this human should and should not do are of course never self-evident. There exists a long list of rather diverse and contradictory injunctions issued by various philosophical and religious traditions, rooted in specific ideas with regard to the order of the universe and the human's place and role in it. It is not my ambition to arbitrate over those injunctions. I also aim to keep adding to this list to the minimum. To offset many moralizing aspects of such injunctions, the ethics presented here is therefore itself positioned as minimal, even though it operates at such large planetary and geological scales. It inscribes itself in "the philosophy of 'less than'" (Morton 2010: 119). As Morton puts it, "Seeing the Earth from space is the beginning of ecological thinking. The first aeronauts, balloon pilots, immediately saw Earth as an alien world. Seeing yourself from another point of view is the beginning of ethics and politics" (2010: 14). Paradoxical as it sounds, the minimal injunction presented here is to think big, perhaps as big as we can, and then to issue the smallest injunctions possible that will allow us to avoid a moralist trap. It is also to consider the philosophical and material possibility of human interconnectedness with other beings—and with cosmic matter itself—but also to see the human him/herself as one more temporary cut made into the flow of matter.

Any such cuts into matter most often occur outside and beyond human consciousness, yet their recognition becomes vital in the production of the historically specific practice called philosophy—and especially ethics. This latter statement gets us out of the dilemma of whether nonhuman animals can also think, perhaps in more complex ways than we realize. Deep skepticism with regard to the uniqueness of human faculties does not mean denying the specificity of descriptive and normative cultural articulations by the human—even if we are to agree that culture is just biology with a shorter time-span. The difference of time difference, or thinking responsibly across and within different scales, is precisely what the minimal ethics for the Anthropocene outlined here stands for.

Notes

15. Steve Shaviro's edited book, *Cognition and Decision in Non-Human Biological Organisms*, provides a helpful account of the problem of decision-as-reaction. His introduction to the volume is an excellent attempt to throw non-humanist light on our conventional ways of understanding such human-centric notions as thinking, decision-making and free will.

16. This point is most cogently argued by Jacques Derrida in "The Animal That Therefore I Am (More to Follow)".

17. I have previously described this kind of argument, which can be seen, among others, in the work of such moral philosophers as John Finnis, John Harris and Peter Singer, as merely postulating a "stretched scale of personhood" (see Zylinska 2009: 11-17).

18. Mullarkey is careful, however, not to suggest an all-the-way equivalence between the two thinkers, insisting that it is equally important to ponder the differences between them. He writes: "Bergson's philosophy of life is too ontological for Levinas, too creative and active. Creation itself presupposes something more fundamental, according to Levinas, namely the revelation of human alterity. The philosophy of the *élan* is flawed because 'it tends toward an impersonal pantheism'. This charge is undoubtedly true: Bergsonism is not a humanism but primarily a philosophy of time extended to all being. Levinas' humanism is wrapped up in his phenomenology, for he clearly views time anthropologically in its essence [...] Without being rationalist, Levinas' primacy of the subjective still remains classical in as much as it

disregards the value of non-human forms of life. [...] however, Bergson's anti-reductionism extends his vision of ethical irreducibility beyond the human psyche towards anything that genuinely endures" (110).

Fig. 9: Joanna Zylinska, *Topia daedala* 9, 2014

Chapter 8

Poetics

If we humans have a singular responsibility to give an account of the differentiations of matter, of which we are part, such practices of account-giving establish a constitutive link between ethics and poetics. Indeed, we encounter ethics precisely via stories and images, i.e., through textual and visual narratives—from sacred texts, works of literature and iconic paintings through to various sorts of media stories and images. It is in this sense, inherited from the Greeks, that products of human creative activity assembled under the general umbrella of "art" perform a *poietic* function: they bring forth realities, concepts and values. Art can therefore be described as world-making rather than just representational. Understood as the supposed "sixth mass extinction of species in the history of life on Earth" (Heise 2010: 49), the Anthropocene acquires its meanings and values through certain types of artistic, or, more broadly, cultural interventions, both written and visual ones, most of which inscribe themselves in what Ursula Heise has described as "the rhetoric of decline". In Heise's words,

Many of these works deploy the genre conventions of elegy and tragedy to construct narratives in which the endangerment or demise of a particular species functions not only as a synecdoche for the broader environmentalist idea of the decline of nature, but also comes to form part of stories that individual cultures tell about their own modernization. (52)

My aim here is to explore several such apocalyptic narratives while also turning to some alternative creative interventions that allow us to reimagine life, death and extinction beyond the narrow fatalism and also beyond what we might term the "rescuism" of the dominant Anthropocene story.

Demise and apocalypse seem to bring with themselves their own pleasures. Indeed, recent years have seen the proliferation of what might be best described as "extinction porn". Stephen's Emmott's book *One Billion* cited in the first chapter would be a good example of this genre; the TV series *Life after People* aired on History channel in 2008-2010 would be another. Each of the twenty episodes of *Life after People* starts with the ominous sounding line: "Welcome to Earth... Population: 0". Viewers are then presented with a situation whereby all humans on Earth have become extinct, even though the program does not go into detail with regard to how this state of events has come about. We are merely faced with this still seemingly fresh and raw status quo, the disappearance of humans from Earth. Interestingly, each episode returns to the very same zero point of "just after the extinction" to then present us with a timescale of several thousand years, showing us different types of urban and biological decay occurring at different times—from the LA freeway system being overgrown with grass to the collapse of the John Hancock Center building in Chicago. This freshly human-free world is nevertheless exactly like we know it: there are no signs of any environmental, planetary or political catastrophe. In *Life after People* humans just seem to have been lifted off by an imaginary spaceship to a different planet, having left their surroundings exactly as we know them. At the same time, the program is actually full of humans, in the shape of various kinds of experts (including some bona fide scientists, such the British geologist and specialist of the Anthropocene Jan Zalasiewicz),[19] who humor the production team by engaging in their own dreamy speculations about how long it will take for various man- and non-man-made bits of the environment to fall apart. All this is accompanied by state-of-the-art computer simulations of collapsing buildings and overgrown cityscapes, seemingly transmitting the message from that other media-friendly scientist, Dr. John Hammond from the *Jurassic Park* sequel: "life will find a way".

The impressive computer graphics and animations in the series create a twenty-first century version of the sublime, with significant historical monuments such as the Sistine Chapel, the Washington Monument and Lenin's Mausoleum, as well as smaller places and objects we hold dear, literally collapsing in front of our eyes. The "in front of our eyes" aspect of the

presentation is of course very important, as this program about life *after people* is aimed at the *very much
present people,* positioned in front of their different
screens to watch with horror the repeated violation
of all the things they have created and value through
the period they refer to as "history". As a result of
various political developments, media audiences in
recent years have been repeatedly exposed to images
of tall buildings collapsing on their screens, thus being
made to witness a new kind of "real screen trauma".
The distantiation effect created through these kinds
of televisual maneuvers is important when it comes
to looking at these overbearing images that inscribe
themselves in the logic and aesthetic of the sublime.
Kant claims that sublime landscapes "raise the forces
of the soul above the height of vulgar commonplace,
and discover within us a power of resistance of quite
another kind, which gives us courage to be able to
measure ourselves against the seeming omnipotence
of nature"—but they do this only "provided our
own position is secure" (110). The repetition of the
trauma of extinction and the ensuing annihilation of
the various monuments of human ingenuity in each
episode of *Life after People* is aimed at shaking up the
people on the other side of the screen while simultaneously restoring their sense of wholeness, control
and peace, thus allowing them to enjoy the spectacle.
Indeed, pleasure—which is the other key component
of the sublime, alongside horror—is very much part
of the experience. It springs from the relief which is
related to the fact of survival, of surmounting the
near-death experience one has been made to witness

but not really be part of. *Life after People* thus holds the Anthropocene at bay, foreclosing on the exploration of any ethico-political issues it potentially brings up. In the last instance, the series only restores and strengthens the anthropos, who gave the name to this geological period—the same way gory horror movies do. Narcissism, self-interest and self-comfort thus overshadow any possibility of the emergence of an ethical response and ethical responsibility in relation to the predicted events. Retold in each episode, like a computer game, from the same starting point and according to the same visual algorithm, the story of the Anthropocene according to *Life after People* is ultimately nothing more than a celebration of human grandeur and thus a futile exercise in triumphalist survivalism.

Such exercises in survivalism, underpinned by human hubris as a supposedly optimal response to the horror of extinction and individual death, have now travelled from the armchairs of media audiences enjoying all sorts of cinematic apocalypses to the labs of bio-resurrectionists. Positioning itself as being part of the wider conservation movement, the resurrection biology project, aka de-extinction or species revivalism, has gained particular attention over recent years thanks to the concerted efforts to bring back the passenger pigeon (Ectopistes migratorius), which became extinct in the early twentieth century. There has also been talk of reviving mammoths. Yet, as pointed out in the *Scientific American* editorial on the issue, "A program to restore extinct species poses a risk of selling the public on a false promise that

technology alone can solve our ongoing environmental woes—an implicit assurance that if a species
goes away, we can snap our fingers and bring it back"
(non-pag.). Positioning organisms as singular entities
that can be "re-inserted" into various environments
rather than as mutually constituted with them, the
de-extinction program sidesteps the broader issue of
our responsibility towards the bio- and geo-sphere by
focusing on individualistic successes of the survival
and revival of "charismatic megafauna" (Heise 2010:
60): the useful and the cute. Suffering precisely from
the derangement of scale critiqued in chapter two
as well as overlooking the complex multi-scalar relations and processes that shape cross-species populations, it reduces any efforts to supposedly "conserve"
and bring back certain species to a human exercise
in species vanity, a capital-fuelled effort to beget life
in a godlike manner. Matter is deprived here of any
vitality of its own and reduced to a mere substrate for
human creation, albeit one that requires a good dose
of venture capital for this process of creation to be car-
ried through.

What else can we do with matter, in its crudest
forms? How can we reinvent life (and death) otherwise, beyond the instrumental, the narcissistic and the
pointless? I would like to see these as more than just
technical questions that call for an engineering solution. Instead, in what follows I want to explore the
practical possibility of bending raw matter in order to
create things, of twisting, turning and splicing matter,
of overcoming its resistance—in a way that exceeds
the rather conservative efforts of bio-resurrectionists.

With this, I want to take issue with the reductionism of many scientific endeavors to either resurrect life or create it from scratch (for example, in the recent experiments in synthetic biology), with life being reduced to sequences of data that can be easily embedded in different media. Life here is basically another version of "the soul". This kind of logic underpins the de-extinction project, especially its dominant section that promotes extracting DNA fragments from preserved specimens and implanting them in the live species (such as band-tailed pigeons) who would become surrogate parents. The disembodied view of information as reducible to the essence of life remains burdened with the metaphysical baggage of the previous centuries, including the dualist distinctions between mind and body, materialism and idealism, transcendence and immanence.

This dualism is poignantly reflected in the words of the popular culture icon, wise man Yoda, in *Star Wars V: The Empire Strikes Back*: "Life creates it, makes it grow. Its energy surrounds us and binds us. Luminous beings are we, not this crude matter". Crude matter is clearly the opposite of life here; it is seen as something that needs an external intervention, a spark, an intelligence, or perhaps just an injection of Craig Venter's capital, to make it alive. In this famous opera of cosmic good and evil, crude matter is presented as *just crude*: inert, unintelligent, dead. Yet what if we were to redeem crude matter as a site of potentiality while at the same time bringing back materiality to the problem of life creation? Leaving behind the mammoth or the pigeon, I would like to turn to the Judaic figure of the Golem as a living being made from mud that approximates, but also potentially threatens, its creator. I suggest we can see the Golem's wisdom and practice as that of an anti-Yoda: as a reclamation of crude matter that always already inheres a potentiality but also as an abandonment of an idea of a "something else". Indeed, the Golem can teach us how to get our hands and minds dirty with the matter of matter, how to think and play with it, and thus with ourselves and our surroundings, in order to think and make life better.

I come to the Golem story and the way it engages with the matter of crude matter via the artistic practice of the Australian duo Oron Catts and Ionat Zurr, who, at the University of Western Australia, have set up a laboratory called SymbioticA and a research initiative called the Tissue Culture and Art Project. In a presentation given in Prague in 2013—a city in which the famous Rabbi Loew ben Bezalel is said to have created a Golem in order to defend the Prague ghetto against pogroms and anti-Semitic attacks— the artists pointed to an emergence of an interesting phenomenon in recent academic discussions in the domains of cultural studies, media theory and art. While life is being increasingly instrumentalized and isolated from its original context to become a product for human manipulation, matter—whether living, semi living or non-living—is attributed with vitality and agency. This philosophical trend, inspired by the work of Gilles Deleuze, Manuel de Landa, Jane Bennett and others, has gained the name "new materialism". For Catts and Zurr this phenomenon "blurs the perceptual (and technological) boundaries between what we consider living, semi living and non-living" (2013: non-pag.).

One of Catts and Zurr's recent art works, which, like their previous pieces, is an attempt to explore precisely this instability between the living, the semi-living and the non-living, is actually titled *Crude Matter*. The piece is concerned with the importance of substrate—that is context—for life. Drawing on current biology research, Catts and Zurr argue that context is as vital to the development of life and its differentiation as genetic code. Referencing the paper "Substrate stiffness affects early differentiation events in embryonic stem cells" by Evans *et al.*, they point out that differentiation of stem cells depends very much on the extra-cellular matrices on which cells grow. Even a subtle change in substrate consistency will have a fundamental effect on the plasticity of cells and the lineage they will take—i.e., on what type of tissue they will become: fat, bone, etc. This is the science that underpins their *Crude Matter* project, which is loosely based on the story of the Golem. The artists explain the project in following terms:

> We are exploring the "alchemy like" transformation of materials into active substrates which have the ability to act as surrogates and upon life. The story of the Golem described the emergence of life from inanimate matter (mud); life that was forceful but brute and could be precariously shaped for different purposes and

intentions. Some say that the body (or the clay dust remains) is still in the attic of the New Old Synagogue of Prague. Our aim is to explore, in a poetic way, and bring back into the forefront the materiality of life in context. This is to differ from the hegemony of the metaphor of life as a code, and the following postulation that life can be controlled. Drawing on historical references taken from the middle ages, we would like to look at engineered life that is on the edges of the what we consider animate or in animate—and provide it with some sort of agency, even if symbolic. (2013: non-pag.)

Their *Crude Matter* installation, shown at KGLU Gallery in Slovenj Gradec, Slovenia, and Łaźnia Centre for Contemporary Art in Gdańsk, Poland, in 2012 is made up from local mud, ceramics, synthetic grass, tissues grown on the PDMS substrate and micro-channels imprinted on glass. The artists aim to dig out soil from historically significant places (the banks of the Vltava (Moldau) river in Prague—from which, according to the legend, the Golem was formed, and a 1942 crash site of a German Junker 88 bomber in the very far north of Finland) and grow life from it, while also allowing it to die—thus trying to understand the relationship between cells and their environment. They claim that the piece "destabilises the engineering logic of the transformation of life into raw material" while also challenging the privileging of the information embedded in DNA over the context in which life operates. "*Crude Matter* is touching upon the creation of life from crude matter and human knowledge; when human hubris and life should not mixed", they say.[20] The work of Catts and Zurr poses the question of what we can we do with crude matter in a way that would take issue with the humanism implied by this very query (as human agency over some external and inchoate mass is claimed up-front), while also remaining critical of the human hubris that underpins many of our contemporary Golem projects, especially those in the corporate biotech world. Indeed, Catts and Zurr are equally interested in what crude matter can do *with* us and *to* us while also revealing that matter is not and has never been just "crude", even though it has suited us humans to imagine it in this way. Instead, matter has been other than itself, or, to use another recently popular term, "relational".

There are a number of other artists (associated with the label "bioart" the way Catts and Zurr also are) whose work takes this relational and contextual approach to the question of life and its locatedness in—and emergence from—matter. Bioart, or a genre of art that engages with life in its fleshy, material way, is an area in which life is being put to the test, beyond any instrumental or reparatory ambitions.[21] In one of their earlier project, Catts and Zurr grew a "semi-living coat" out of immortalized cell lines, which formed a living layer of tissue supported by a biodegradable polymer matrix. Displayed in a glass sphere connected to various test tubes, the tiny garment-like object, branded *Victimless Leather*, brings to the fore, in their own words, "the moral implications of wearing parts of dead animals for protective and aesthetic reasons",[22] while also engaging us in a visceral reflection on our use of living systems in everyday life. Another example of enacting the relationality of matter otherwise is a project called *Blender* by Australian artists Stelarc and Nina Sellars. *Blender* is a vibrant installation consisting of a large glass capsule in which liquid biomaterial (such as subcutaneous fat from both artists' bodies, obtained via liposuction) bubbles and sloshes about, accompanied by the regular clicking sound of the blending mechanism's switch, which creates a pulse-like effect. Life's effervescence is poignantly embraced in Eduardo Kac's "plantimal" *Edunia*—a handsomely growing genetically engineered pinkish flower which is a hybrid of the artist and a petunia, with the artist's own DNA expressed in the red veins traversing the petals.

Yet I want to suggest that it is not so much its daring or even blasphemous novelty that makes bioart worth our attention. Rather, it is *what happens to life itself* within bioartistic practice that opens up the most interesting set of possibilities—for artists, philosophers, scientists, engineers and a wider public. These possibilities are not just visual but also material, and thus we may say, ontological: they concern the very nature of existence in time, and of what we understand by the seemingly self-evident concepts such as intelligence; sex and reproduction; the body; and the very concept of being alive. In works such as those by the Tissue Culture and Art Project, Stelarc and Sellars or Kac life is being re-created, pushed to the limit, remolded, remediated, cut and spliced back again. Bioartists can thus be said to take art's creative imperative to a different level, echoing to an extent what Bergson termed "creative evolution"—a form of life's unfolding which does not proceed in straight vertical lines according to a pre-designed formula but which rather entails the possibility of creating some "real novelty", or what Sarah Kember has termed "life-as-it-could-be" (2006: non-pag.). This is not to say that novelty is desirable under any circumstances, or that it is inherently progressive and good. Nor is it to assert that bioart remains outside the dominant cultural norms, or that the creative impulse which underpins their practice releases artists involved in the manipulation of life at genetic, cellular or tissue level from wider social conventions and obligations. We should therefore by all means give due consideration to questions concerning artists' rights and moral obligations that frequently get raised in debates surrounding bioart: questions as to whether artists *have the right* to create and manipulate life and to "play God" the way Rabi Loeb did with his Prague Golem made out of the soil of the Vltava river, whether *it is "moral"* to do so, and whether *life as such does not deserve some kind of protection* from the possible excesses of some irresponsible experimenters—excesses that the twentieth century in particular witnessed in high number.

However, I also want to suggest that the most important work of invention undertaken by many bioartists occurs not so much on an ontological level but rather on an ethical one. We could perhaps go so far as to suggest that artistic experiments of this kind furnish what might be described as an "ethics lab", whereby it is not just life that is experimented on but also the normative frameworks through which it can be approached and dealt with. If acting ethically involves making cuts to the flow of life, as I suggested in chapter three, then we need to acknowledge that those cuts are going to be both material (involving the cutting and splicing of genes or cells) and rhetorical. In performing (bio)ethics with their work, bioartists seem to be taking heed of Deleuze and Guattari's philosophical imperative to approach problems of the world not just by saying what we already know about it but first of all by inventing new concepts—a process which for the authors of *What Is Philosophy?* is a "matter of articulation, of cutting and cross-cutting" (1994: 16). Bioart can thus be described as being involved in the twin processes of inventing life and cutting through life—with a double-edged scalpel of responsibility and necessity. This is to say that cutting, both material and rhetorical, is inevitable, but also that the kinds of incisions that we are going to make into life matter. Indeed, they matter also in an ethical sense, which will have to be decided anew in various contexts. Since this nebulous entity called "life" is itself in the process of being re/created in the artistic experiments and their articulations, there is of course no reason to posit "life" as a value in advance. As Rosi Braidotti argues, life is a "fundamentally amoral force, the true nature of which is best expressed in its relentless generative power. There is no implicit a priori difference between cancer and birth, or between a malignant proliferation of cells in cancer and the benign proliferation induced by pregnancy" (2006: 223). Seeing life as a force, a dynamic movement, an unfolding of potentialities which are often unknown in advance carries with it both a suspension of ontological certainty and an ethical imperative to cut well into life, to make good things with it. Rather than posited as a prior value, life becomes a minimum condition of any ethical framework—and of there being those who can exercise and act on that condition. To cite Braidotti again, "Ethics is a thin barrier against the possibility of extinction. It is a mode of actualizing sustainable forms of transformation" (217). It is therefore the protection of this condition, of the possibility of life's unfolding—but not necessarily a protection of this or that life form—that constitutes a minor injunction for our ethics for the Anthropocene. This injunction always needs to be coupled with two others: to cut well into life and to respond well to life already formed (or, as we may also put it, "temporarily stabilized"): to entities, beings, organs, cells—as well as elephants and band-tailed pigeons that are still with us. It also means taking responsibility for the life of the other, be it another human, a Golem or a slime mold, but not necessarily in the same way.

The imperative to "invent well" is derived from humans' capacity for developing empathy with other life forms, for being sentient with and about them, and for being able to theorize this shared sentience. However, it is precisely the moment of reflection on that capacity and the forms of affect it generates that is a condition for any such living encounter being ethical. (Otherwise there is a danger of cuteness or media-induced charisma becoming a moral value.) We could therefore suggest that bioartists, busying themselves in their "ethics labs," are twenty-first century science-philosophers, who, like Rabbi Loew with his Golem, are both making life and making rules about life. But they do need to take responsibility for their own situatedness in life: for their engagement with matter and for their differentiation from it. Of course, not all bioartists are ethical in this sense, with many reneging on their minimal "critical vitalist imperative" to create life and to reflect on it. But the interesting even if rare examples of "good invention" can turn bioart into an important tester of our moral hierarchies — of how we value certain life forms more than others, and of how we cut through matter, to make life better.

Notes

19. Zalasiewicz's publications on the Anthropocene include a co-authored chapter "Anthropocene" in *A Geologic Time Scale* and a book, *The Earth After Us: The Legacy That Humans Will Leave In The Rocks.*

20. Project description for the Crude Matter exhibition at KGLU Gallery in Slovenj Gradec, Slovenia, 2012, http://kiblix.org/kiblix2012/softcontrol/?p=103.

21. The material on bioart included in the last third of this chapter has been adopted from Joanna Zylinska. "Taking Responsibility for Life: Bioethics and Bioart". In: Paul Macneill (ed.) *Ethics and the Arts*. Series: Library of Ethics and Applied Philosophy/ LOET. Amsterdam: Springer, 2014.

22. The Tissue Culture and Art Project website,
    http://www.tca.uwa.edu.au/vl/vl.html, accessed
    January 20, 2014.

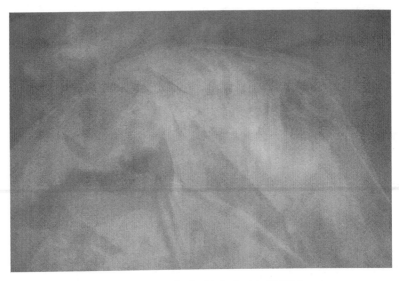

Fig. 10: Joanna Zylinska, *Topia daedala* 10, 2014

Chapter 9

Politics

Hopefully by now the reader has a sense that the Anthropocene is a really serious matter, one that requires our attention as both critical theorists and living, breathing organism that are preoccupied—and that ought to be preoccupied—on an intellectual and a visceral level, with ensuring the continued possibility of life. I am referring here both to individual life and to the life of whole populations, or even species. This ethical injunction therefore immediately opens up onto a political task, one that involves having to negotiate between conflicting demands, work through antagonisms arising from opposite and sometimes even irreconcilable positions, and calculate between various options available to us. To say this is to counter the accusation issued by certain political philosophers that ethics is just a replacement problem, or even an individualized neoliberal strategy that prevents us from analyzing bigger issues, planning collective action and working against injustice or catastrophes on a global level. Indeed, my argument here (as in my previous work) is that ethics must be *foundational* to politics: it needs to prepare the ground for political work in which responsibilities are always shared and demands conflicting. Unless we engage in the work of ethics that involves a reflection on our own constitution of values, we run the risk of unreformed moralism being passed off as politics. I would go so far as to say that there can be no political urgency urgent enough that could serve as a justification for abandoning the foundational and structural work of ethics. Many political projects of different orientation have failed precisely because of their proponents' inability, or unwillingness, to reflect on the constitution of their own values: their idea of justice and "good", their clamor for a "better tomorrow"—which is likely to be someone else's horizon of horror.

It goes without saying that the Anthropocene presents itself to us as a political problem, but it does require at least a minimal dose of ethical reflection if a politics it is to usher in is to be both truly effective and truly political. The constitution of this kind of ethical reflection in preparation for a more considerate and more effective politics of the Anthropocene is precisely the ambition of this book, even if, or in fact precisely because of the fact that, this term carries a certain geo-temporal urgency. Minimal ethics for the Anthropocene is to serve as a caution against understanding the Anthropocene too well and too quickly, and against knowing precisely how to solve the problems it represents. The task of such minimal ethics, as argued earlier, is to pose the Anthropocene as an ethical injunction. However, this injunction also entails the requirement to remain critical towards the very concept of the Anthropocene and the way it is framed in the current debates, both academic and mainstream ones—not in order to reject it, but in order to develop a more complex and more responsible discourse on the Anthropocene, as well as facilitating a better political response to it. The three issues that require particular attention, as already discussed throughout this book, are the underpinning masculinism, solutionism and scientism of this discourse—all manifested, to return to a quote from Darin Barney included in the first chapter, "the sort of bravado whereby men seek to exert control over everything around them by the force of instrumental rationality" (non-pag.). The interpellation here is not to impose women-only activism, suspend any search for solutions or bash science: it is only to keep a check on some of the excesses that have come to the fore in the debate on the subject to date. The conclusion that emerges from the above is that critical thinking is one of the forms that politics of the Anthropocene can or even has to take. Indeed, perhaps thinking is the most political thing we can do with regard to the Anthropocene, before we go and do anything else. This should not be mistaken for a sign of resignation or quietism in the face of a planetary task. As Dave Boothroyd observes, "Thinking is doing something even if from the outside it looks like doing nothing" (16).

If the Anthropocene raises questions of decay, destruction and death on a much larger, deeper and more significant scale than many of the previous political figurations, such as "the Iron Curtain", "Al-Qaeda" or "globalization", it is also arguably a game changer with regard to the established political models and formats. Indeed, it requires a reworking of the positions, allegiances and frameworks, as well as of some of the fundamental concepts that underpin them, such as freedom, justice and life itself. As pointed out by historian Dipesh Chakrabarty in his by now well-cited article on the Anthropocene,

> Climate change, refracted through global capital, will no doubt accentuate the logic of inequality that runs through the rule of capital; some people will no doubt gain temporarily at the expense of others. But the whole crisis cannot be reduced to a story of capitalism. Unlike in the crises of capitalism, there are no lifeboats here for the rich and the privileged (witness the drought in Australia or recent fires in the wealthy neighborhoods of California). (non-pag.)

Chakrabarty's article is not free from the masculinism and scientism that characterizes many other humanities writers on the Anthropocene, and it ends up reaffirming a reformulated form of humanism, with a sprinkling of old-style liberalism. Yet his analysis does raise the important question of directionality for the left with regard to the critique it forges and the future it envisages—for itself, for humanity and for "the world". The imminent depletion of our planet's reserves, dubbed an "eco-eco disaster" by Tom Cohen, pushes us to revise politics as a matter of "the 'economical and 'ecological' tandem" (2012: 14).

This brings up not just the question of how we can define "a political subject of climate change" (Cohen

2012: 18) who is at the same time a subject of economic injustice, labor scarcity and bad debt, but also the problem of whether we should perhaps remain suspicious towards any attempts to fix a political subject in its identitarian position as a wounded self that can then retroactively respond to a situation. Instead, would a more potent political strategy not need to mobilize a distributed, relational and even partly non-human subjectivity as both its agent and an object of its attention? Cohen suggests that, if we take on board the issue of climate change and the human-led transformation of the geo- and biosphere, what we call the "political" needs to "migrate from an exclusively social category (Aristotle), as it has been defined in relation to the polity, to a cognitive or epistemographic zone" (24). This is to say, the arena of politics has to become much more expanded but it also requires a conscious effort on the part of those of us who want to actively participate in it to relearn and reimagine its geopolitical and geomoral configurations, to see anew where political urgency currently lies. Also, if the Anthropocene is defined as a crisis of scarcity, in the sense that humans are said to have almost used up the existent resources of the planet they call home, it is also worth asking, with Arundhati Roy, "What happens once democracy has been used up?". Speaking from the position of someone who deeply cares about the democratic ideal, she nevertheless offers a damning indictment of its enactment in the so-called global world:

Could it be that democracy is such a hit
with modern humans precisely because it
mirrors our greatest folly—our nearsight-
edness? Our inability to live entirely in
the present (like most animals do) combined with our inability to see very far into
the future makes us strange in-between
creatures, neither beast nor prophet. Our
amazing intelligence seems to have out-
stripped our instinct for survival. We plun-
der the earth hoping that accumulating
material surplus will make up for the pro-
found, unfathomable thing that we have
lost. (non-pag.)

For Roy, the problem lies in the actual strategies we
have used across the globe precisely in the name of
democracy—strategies that have led it to fuse with
the free market into a predatory mechanism whose
sole rationale is the maximization of profit. In India,
which is the focus of her analysis—although the
examples can be extrapolated to other developing
countries too—this has involved making sudden and
drastic decisions with regard to the building of dams,
which has led to the submerging of inhabited lands by
water; massive land acquisitions at gunpoint; the bull-
dozing of acres of living areas; the uncontrolled pol-
lution of rivers and the unprecedented increase in car
use and electronics consumption. While the scarcity
of natural resources, especially fossil fuels, is a familiar line of argument with regard to the Anthropocene,
Roy points to something that may initially sound

counter-intuitive: namely, that the very political framework that underpins the foundational notions of democracy such as popular sovereignty, political equality and freedom to choose political representation may have become exhausted through its overexploitation by the demands of the global and local market. Uncared for, democracy is reduced into a mere shadow of its former self, serving mainly the interests of those who do not really care enough, or even understand what it means to care, about the future of the polis in all its bio- and geo-political dimensions.

However, there is a certain paradox at work in trying to combat the political self-interest that has got us to where we are. It lies in the fact that many efforts to respond to the Anthropocene actually mobilize a certain notion of speciecist, or more precisely humanist, self-interest—to combat self-interest! Political theorist Jane Bennett is aware of this problem but remains unapologetic when she asks: "*Should* we try to detach geologic sensibility from *all* notions of self-interest? Is it really possible, given our current evolutionary form, to live according to the maxim that 'while the human species can't get along without the geologic, the geologic will continue on in some form or other long after we have ceased being part of it?'" (2012: 246). This is of course a pertinent query, one that drives many current scientific and philosophical efforts to respond to the supposed urgency of the current geopolitical moment in order to ensure a better life, politically and biologically, for both ourselves and the future generations, and to prolong that life in the shape and form that is considered more sustainable or even salutary at both micro and macro scales. However, it may also be worth asking what it means for a politics of the Anthropocene to be principally driven by species narcissism, or a desire for human survival? How will it differ from some of the worst excesses of materialist politics, whereby the definition of materialism is less Epicureanist and more Gordon Geckoist? To put it really crudely—and perhaps also unfairly to Bennett, whose own political orientations lie very much on the left—how do we ensure her position is differentiated from pronouncements such as those by Conservative politician and London mayor Boris Johnson, who, as reported by *The Guardian*, in the 2013 Margaret Thatcher lecture "mocked the 16% 'of our species' with an IQ below 85 as he called for more to be done to help the 2% of the population who have an IQ above 130". Johnson said: "Whatever you may think of the value of IQ tests it is surely relevant to a conversation about equality that as many as 16% of our species have an IQ below 85 while about 2% ... The harder you shake the pack the easier it will be for some cornflakes to get to the top".[23] Indeed, if this desire for survival is seen as primarily natural (as this is how we have *evolved*, according to Bennett), how will we guarantee it does not result in the short-termism of goal and the return to organicism she is so keen to escape otherwise? Does her acknowledgement in *Vibrant Matter* that she shares Epicureanist monism's "conviction that there remains a natural *tendency* to the way things are—and that human decency and a decent politics are fostered if we tune in to the strange logic of turbulence" (2010: xi) not assume the existence of a whole group of some rather nice people who will all agree in advance, by *tendency*, osmosis or just through their plain good upbringing, what "human decency" is and what a "decent politics" will look like?

Indeed, I would risk saying that Bennet's politics is not political enough because it forecloses on the examination of narcissism, or, more broadly—its own affective investment in the idea of survival, life as energy and vibrant matter—at the heart of politics. While I agree with her that "Affirming the geo-mode of long time also holds promise for lifting American political discourse above its currently idiocy, wherein crucial issues like climate change are elided for the sake of moralistic red herrings or theo-populist slogans" (2012: 245), I am more concerned about the moralism of eco-eco politics. Indeed, I fear that it may end up reducing any political efforts to self-interest on a mega scale, while also remaining inattentive to the cuts, small interventions (made also by, but mainly to, those "idiotic Americans" with their idiotic discourses, not the nice decent people who all agree on the idea of human decency) with regard to their current situation, both geographical and socio-economic. I wonder whether what Bennett ends up proposing, together with many other theorists of critical environment studies—even those who have gone to great lengths to raise questions for the established ideas of "nature" and "the environment"—is not just a politics for those who like (deconstructed) nature a lot, with matter becoming "the new nature". The politics of vibrant matter therefore risks looking like a middle-class affectation, one aimed at people who read critical theory but also have a preference for organic food, shop at farmer's markets, like getting out of the city now and again, and generally are "anti-consumerist": basically, nice affluent moralists who are doing their bit for the planet while also suffering not just from derangements of scale but also derangements of their own decency. Incidentally, the notion of decency is one evoked most frequently by the UK Conservative party, whose aim is to "help you and hardworking people in your area".[24]

Now, I absolutely agree with Bennett and other theorists of nonantropocentric thought about the need to perceive agency as distributed amongst human and nonhuman actors, some of whom/which are unstable and difficult to see (by us), and thus to recognize that our own belief in the possibility of controlling every aspect of the unfolding matter is nothing but a delusion. Indeed, unless we take into account the agential force of nonhuman phenomena and objects, we risk being unable to truly intervene into things. Yet it also seems to me that the politics for the Anthropocene will have to come to terms with what Chantal Mouffe has called "the democratic paradox"—for which there is no room in Bennett's flat ontologies. The democratic paradox signifies that the liberal democratic idea of "human rights," for example, if applied to its logical conclusion, will always inevitably jeopardize someone else's existing rights. Mouffe emphasizes that it is important for us to understand that in a liberal democracy there always exists "a constitutive tension" between different logics, grammars or articulations (say, of ideas of God, freedom, nature, justice, property, dignity, etc.), "a tension that can never be overcome but only negotiated in different ways" (5). Mouffe does not naïvely advocate any kind of straightforward resolution of such tension premised on a liberal rational argument as the latter will inevitably entail its own constitutive blind spots, but rather offers (discursive, but perhaps also bodily—i.e., involving the opponent's gestures, breath, spit) "contamination" as the best resolution we can hope for (10).

When talking about articulation here we are back in a somewhat constrained realm of human discourse, but at the same time we have to acknowledge humans' constant and ongoing entanglement with other entities and processes. I am therefore happy to borrow from Bennett the notion of "political ecologies" and to acknowledge, with her, "nonhuman materialities as participants in a political ecology". Importantly, Bennett herself goes to great trouble not to claim "that everything is always a participant, or that all participants are alike". Indeed, she insists that "Persons, worms, leaves, bacteria, metals, and hurricanes have different types and degrees of power" (2010: 108). However, even if "A vital materialist theory of democracy seeks to transform the divide between speaking subjects and mute objects into a set of differential tendencies and variable capacities" (2010: 107-8), questions arise with regard to the *inadequately theorized* (even if not unacknowledged)[25] moments of articulation on the part of the materialist philosopher who speaks *about* and *for* other actors. The problem here is that the philosopher has already claimed his or her articulatory ground: by philosophizing, in the rather conventional humanist medium of the book (most often made of dead trees, no less!), about things that have already been muted once they have been constituted as objects of discourse, especially if the relations into which they have been made to enter include notions such as decency, sustainability and vigor. What is therefore troubling for me about all this is the lack of *adequate* examination on the part of the many philosophers of materialism and materiality of their own affective investment in, as well as of their role in constituting, the discourse about politics.

Even the apparently hospitable and generous gesture of opening up the political ecology to other actors is enacted from the position of the established practice of philosophical exegesis—while remaining constrained by uninterrogated notions such as "decency" and "vibrancy". Consequently, "there still lingers the notion of, and a longing for, a present underlying foundation and/or truth in some political and theoretical movements and writings" (Bruining 2013: 150),[26] even or maybe especially those that explicitly disavow any such foundationalism. Indeed, even though matter for Bennett entails violent tendencies, her description of it is like that of a really lovely and bubbly friend: Bennettian matter is "vital, energetic, lively, quivering, vibratory, evanescent, and effluescent" (Bennett 2010: 112)—very much unlike the life-draining, low-in-energy, cantankerous, old-school critical theorist who can only find problems with things... The more substantial issue with this approach lies not in the recognition of the existence of matter as such but rather in what Dennis Bruining has termed "material foundationalism", an approach "in which matter translates and comes to signify an exigency of life" (149). In works of so-called "new materialism" such as Bennett's matter tends to be posited as "a priori and as, allegedly, beyond culture, despite an awareness of the untenability of such claims" (Bruining 2013: 151). Yet the positing of such matter can only be premised on the simultaneous occlusion of the humanist values that underpin such a philosophical "positing gesture"—not to mention the reintroduction of the old-style Cartesianism, except that now the principal driver of agency is on the side of "matter" rather than "the mind" (see Bruining 2013: 158).

Another problem with this new "rediscovered" matter and all its posited foundationalism is that it assumes a community of those who call themselves human who supposedly experience and "feel" it strongly enough, in the sense that relationality across strata and scales becomes *meaningful* enough for them as something to shape their world-view—rather than as something, say, too overwhelming, too general or even too banal to consider. In the same way that it is much easier to "do animal studies" if you really "like" animals (even though the latter position can lead to the similar kind of moralizing critiqued in this chapter and end up producing positions that are actually anti-philosophical), it is much easier to "do materialist ecopolitics" if you feel energized by (all kind of talk of) matter.

To close off this chapter I would therefore like to propose the possibility of outlining a politics for the Anthropocene from a different place than species narcissism or enthusiastically sensed materialist affinity with things "out there", across the universe. We can call it an ironic politics for city lovers—for those for whom matter is not a bubbly friend, for whom "it" does not move just like "wind" (120) but more like a Porsche, and for whom philosophizing, storytelling and art-making function as inevitable *technical* prostheses for a human engaged in the theorization of matter—or, indeed, in the theorization of anything else.

Notes

23. http://www.theguardian.com/politics/2013/nov/27/boris-johnson-thatcher-greed-good, accessed December 2, 2013.

24. http://www.conservatives.com/, accessed December 2, 2013.

25. Indeed, Bennett self-consciously comments: "I court the charge of performative self-contradiction: is it not a human subject who, after all, is articulating this theory of vibrant matter? Yes and no, for I will argue that what looks like a performative contradiction may well dissipate if one considers revisions in operative notions of matter, life, self, self-interest, will, and agency" (2010: ix).

26. Bruining is drawing here on Wendy Brown.

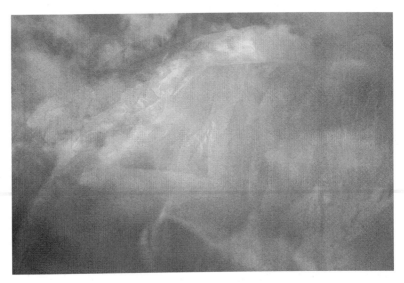

Fig. 11: Joanna Zylinska, *Topia daedala* 11, 2014

Chapter 10

Manifesting

Tom Cohen suggests that in the Anthropocene era "writing practices might be apprehended in their interweave with carbon and hydro-carbon accelerations, from a position *beyond mourning* and the automatisms of personification, or 'identification'" (25). It is precisely in this affirmative spirit that I round off this book with a biopoetic manifesto for a minimal ethics against all odds, outlined in twenty-one theses:

1. The universe is constantly unfolding but it also temporarily stabilizes into entities.

2. None of the entities in the universe are pre-planned or necessary.

3. Humans are one class of entities in the universe, which is as accidental and transitory as any other class.

4. The differentiation between process and entity is a heuristic, but it allows us to develop a discourse about the world and about ourselves in that world.

5. The world is an imaginary name we humans give to the multitude of unfoldings of matter.

6. Transitory stabilizations of matter do matter
   to us humans, but they do not all matter in
   the same way.

7. Ethics is a historically contingent human mode
   of becoming in the world—and of becoming
   different from the world.

8. Ethics is therefore stronger than ontology:
   it entails becoming-something in response
   to there being something else, even though
   this "something else" is only a temporary
   stabilization.

9. This response is not just discursive but also
   affective and corporeal.

10. Ethics is necessary because it is inevitable: we
    humans must respond to there being other
    processes and other entities in the world.

11. Our response is a way of taking responsibility
    for the multiplicity of the world, and for our
    relations to and with it.

12. Such responsibility can always be denied or
    withdrawn, but a response will have already
    taken place nonetheless.

13. Responsibility is not just a passive reaction to
    pre-existing reality: it involves actively making
    cuts into the ongoing unfolding of matter in
    order to stabilize it.

14. Material in-cisions undertaken by humans can
    be ethical de-cisions, even if the majority of
    such cuts into matter are nothing of the kind.

15. Even if ethics is inevitable, ethical events are rare.

16. Ethics requires an account of itself.

17. Ethics precedes politics but also makes a demand on the political as the historically specific order of sometimes collaborative and sometimes competitive relations between human and nonhuman entities.

18. As a practice of material and conceptual differentiation, ethics entails violence, but it should also work towards minimizing violence.

19. There is therefore value in ethics, even if ethics itself needs no prior values.

20. Ethics is a critical mobilization of the creative principle of life in order to facilitate a good life.

21. Ethics enables the production of better modes of becoming, whose goodness is worked out by humans in the political realm, in relation with, and with regard to, non-human entities and entanglements.

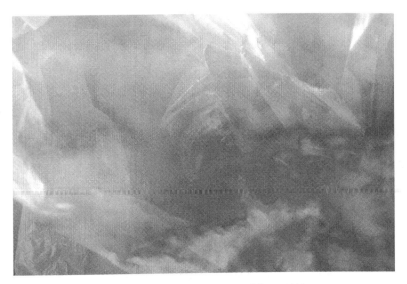

Fig. 12: Joanna Zylinska, *Topia daedala* 12, 2014

Topia daedala, 2014

The series of images included in the book continues my visual exploration of various forms of manufactured landscape. Taken from two vantage points on both sides of a window, the composite images interweave human and nonhuman creativity by overlaying the outer world of cloud formation with the inner space of sculptural arrangement. Remediating the tradition of the sublime as embraced by J.M.W. Turner's landscape paintings and Ansel Adams' national park photographs, the series foregrounds the inherent constructedness of what counts as "landscape" and of the conventions of its visual representation. Through this, *Topia daedala* performs a micro-sublime for the Anthropocene era, a period in which the human has become identified as a geological agent. It also raises questions for the role of plastic—as both construction material and debris—in the age of petrochemical urgency.

Works Cited

Adorno, Theodor. *Minima Moralia: Reflections on a Damaged Life*. Trans. E. F. N. Jephcott. London and New York: Verso, 2005.

Badiou, Alain. *Ethics: An Essay on the Understanding of Evil*. Trans. Peter Hallward. London and New York: Verso, 2001.

Badiou, Alain. *Manifesto for Philosophy*. Trans. Norman Madarasz. Albany: State University of New York Press, 1999.

Badiou, Alain. "On a Finally Objectless Subject". *Who Comes After the Subject?* Ed. Eduardo Cadava, Peter Connor and Jean-Luc Nancy. New York and London: Routledge, 1991. 24-32.

Barad, Karen. *Meeting the Universe Halfway: Quantum Physics and the Entanglement of Matter*. Durham, NC: Duke University Press, 2007.

Barney, Darin. "Eat Your Vegetables: Courage and the Possibility of Politics". *Theory & Event*. 14:2 (Summer 2011). Project MUSE. Web. December 9, 2013. http://muse.jhu.edu/.

Bennett, Jane. "Afterword: Earthling, Now and Forever?" *Making the Geologic Now: Responses to Material Conditions of Contemporary Life*. Ed. Elizabeth Ellsworth and Jamie Kruse. Brooklyn, NY: Punctum Books, 2012.

Bennett, Jane. *Vibrant Matter: A Political Ecology of Things*. Durham and London: Duke University Press, 2010.

Bergson, Henri. *Creative Evolution*. Trans. Arthur Mitchell. New York: Random House, The Modern Library, 1944.

Bergson, Henri. *The Two Sources of Morality and Religion.* Trans. R. Ashley Audra and Cloudesley Brereton. London: MacMillan and Co., 1935.

Boothroyd, Dave. *Ethical Subjects in Contemporary Culture.* Edinburgh: Edinburgh University Press, 2013.

Braidotti, Rosi. *Nomadic Subjects: Embodiment and Sexual Difference in Contemporary Feminist Theory.* New York: Columbia University Press, 1994.

Braidotti, Rosi. *The Posthuman.* Cambridge: Polity, 2013.

Braidotti, Rosi. *Transpositions: On Nomadic Ethics.* Cambridge: Polity Press, 2006.

Brown, Wendy. *Manhood and Politics: A Feminist Reading in Political Theory.* Totowa, NJ: Rowman & Littlefield, 1988.

Brown, Wendy. *Politics Out of History.* Princeton and Oxford: Princeton University Press, 2001.

Bruining, Dennis. "A Somatechnics of Moralism: New Materialism or Material Foundationalism". *Somatechnics* 3.1 (2013): 149–168.

Bryant, Levi R. *The Democracy of Objects.* Ann Arbor: Open Humanities Press, 2011.

Butko, Peter. "*Summa technologiae* – Looking Back and Ahead". *The Art and Science of Stanislaw Lem.* Ed. Peter Swirski. Montreal and Kingston, London, Ithaca: McGill-Queen's University Press, 2006.

Calarco, Matthew. *Zoographies: The Question of the Animal from Heidegger to Derrida.* New York: Columbia University Press, 2008.

Catts, Oron and Ionat Zurr. "Crude Matter: The Milieu as Life Enabling". Presentation at CIANT Prague, 2013, https://vimeo.com/56462011

Chakrabarty, Dipesh. "The Climate of History: Four Theses". *Eurozine*. October 30, 2009. http://www.eurozine.com/ articles/2009-10-30-chakrabarty-en.html. First published in *Critical Inquiry* 35 (Winter 2009): 197-222.

Christian, David. *Maps of Time: An Introduction to Big History*. Berkeley: University of California Press, 2011.

Clark, Timothy. "Derangements of Scale". *Telemorphosis: Theory in the Era of Climate Change*, Vol. 1. Ed. Tom Cohen. Ann Arbor: Open Humanities Press, 2012.

Cohen, Tom. "Introduction: Murmurations – 'Climate Change' and the Defacement of Theory". *Telemorphosis: Theory in the Era of Climate Change*, Vol. 1. Ed. Tom Cohen. Ann Arbor: Open Humanities Press, 2012.

Colebrook, Claire. *Deleuze and the Meaning of Life*. London and New York: Continuum, 2010.

Colebrook, Claire. "Introduction: Framing the End of the Species". *Extinction*. Ed. Claire Colebrook. Living Books About Life series. Ann Arbor: Open Humanities Press, 2012. http://www.livingbooksaboutlife.org/books/ Extinction

Critchley, Simon. "Demanding Approval: On the Ethics of Alain Badiou". *Radical Philosophy* 100 (March-April 2000): 16-27.

Deleuze, Gilles and Félix Guattari. *A Thousand Plateaus: Capitalism and Schizophrenia*. Trans. Brian Massumi. Minneapolis: University of Minnesota Press, 1987.

Deleuze, Gilles and Félix Guattari. *What is Philosophy?* Trans. Hugh Tomlinson and Graham Burchell. New York: Columbia University Press, 1994.

Derrida, Jacques. "Afterword: Toward an Ethic of Discussion". Trans. Samuel Weber. Jacques Derrida, *Limited Inc*. Evanston: Northwestern University Press, 1988.

Derrida, Jacques. *Spurs: Nietzsche's Styles*. Trans. Barbara Harlow. Chicago and London: University of Chicago Press, 1979.

Derrida, Jacques. "The Animal That Therefore I Am (More to Follow)". Trans. David Wills. *Critical Inquiry* 28 (Winter 2002): 369–418.

Derrida, Jacques. "'There is No One Narcissism' (Autobiophotographies)". Jacques Derrida, *Points ... Interview, 1974–1994*. Ed. Elisabeth Weber. Stanford: Stanford University Press, 1995.

Derrida, Jacques and Bernard Stiegler. *Echographies of Television*. Trans. Jennifer Bajorek. Cambridge: Polity Press, 2002.

Eldredge, Niles. "Foreword: Undreamed Philosophies". *What Is Life?* Lynn Margulis and Dorion Sagan. New York: Simon & Schuster, 1995.

Emmott, Stephen. *Ten Billion*. Harmondsworth: Penguin (Kindle edition), 2013.

Gray, John. "Are we Done For?" *The Guardian*. July 6, 2013, 6.

Hallward, Peter. "Ethics without Others: A Reply to Critchley on Badiou's *Ethics*". *Radical Philosophy* 102 (July-August 2000): 27-30.

Haraway, Donna J. *Simians, Cyborgs and Women: The Reinvention of Nature*. London: Free Association Books, 1991.

Haraway, Donna. *The Companion Species Manifesto: Dogs, People, and Significant Otherness*. Chicago: Prickly Paradigm Press, 2003.

Hawking, Stephen. *A Brief History of Time*. New York: Bantam Books, 1988.

Hayles, N. Katherine. "(Un)masking the Agent: Stanislaw Lem's 'The Mask'". *The Art and Science of Stanislaw Lem.* Ed. Peter Swirski. Montreal and Kingston, London, Ithaca: McGill-Queen's University Press, 2006.

Heise, Ursula K. "Lost Dogs, Last Birds, and Listed Species: Cultures of Extinction". *Configurations* 18.102 (Winter 2010): 49-72.

Ingold, Tim. *Being Alive: Essays on Movement, Knowledge and Description.* London: Routledge, 2011.

Ingold, Tim. "Beyond Biology and Culture: The Meaning of Evolution in a Relational World". *Social Anthropology* 12.2 (2004): 209–221.

Jarzębski, Jerzy. "Models of Evolution in the Writings of Stanislaw Lem". *The Art and Science of Stanislaw Lem.* Ed. Peter Swirski. Montreal and Kingston, London, Ithaca: McGill-Queen's University Press, 2006.

Kant, Immanuel. *The Critique of Judgement.* Trans. James Meredith. Oxford: Clarendon Press, 1952.

Kember, Sarah. "Creative Evolution? The Quest for Life (on Mars)". *Culture Machine,* Interzone (March 2006). http://www.culturemachine.net/index.php/cm/article/view/235/216. Accessed July 7, 2011.

Kember, Sarah and Joanna Zylinska. "Media Always and Everywhere: A Cosmic Approach". *Ubiquitous Computing, Complexity and Culture.* Ed. Ulrik Ekman *et al.* New York and London: Routledge, 2015, forthcoming.

Kolbert, Elizabeth. "Enter the Anthropocene – Age of Man". *Making the Geologic Now: Responses to Material Conditions of Contemporary Life.* Ed. Elizabeth Ellsworth and Jamie Kruse. Brooklyn, NY: Punctum Books, 2012. Originally published in *National Geographic* magazine, March 2011.

Lem, Stanisław. *Return from the Stars*. Trans. Barbara Marszal and Frank Simpson. New York: Harcourt Brace, 1980. (1961)

Lem, Stanisław. *Summa Technologiae*. Trans. Joanna Zylinska. Minneapolis: University of Minnesota Press, 2013. (1964)

Levinas, Emmanuel. "Ethics as First Philosophy". *The Levinas Reader*. Ed. Sean Hand. Oxford: Blackwell, 1989.

Levinas, Emmanuel. *Otherwise Than Being: Or Beyond Essence*. Trans. Alphonso Lingis. Pittsburgh: Duquesne University Press, 1998.

Levinas, Emmanuel. *Totality and Infinity: An Essay on Exteriority*. Trans. Alphonso Lingis. Pittsburgh: Duquesne University Press, 1969.

Margulis, Lynn. *Symbiotic Planet: A New Look at Evolution*. New York: Basic Books, 1998.

Margulis, Lynn and Dorion Sagan. *What Is Life?* New York: Simon & Schuster, 1995.

Morton, Timothy. *Ecology without Nature: Rethinking Environmental Aesthetics*. Cambridge, MA: Harvard University Press, 2007.

Morton, Timothy. *The Ecological Thought*. Cambridge, MA: Harvard University Press, 2010.

Mouffe, Chantal. *The Democratic Paradox*. London: Verso, 2000.

Mullarkey, John. *Bergson and Philosophy*. Edinburgh: Edinburgh University Press, 1999.

Plato. "Apology". *Plato in Twelve Volumes*, Vol. 1. Trans. Harold North Fowler; Introduction by W.R.M. Lamb. Cambridge, MA: Harvard University Press; London: William Heinemann Ltd. 1966. Available online at: http://www.perseus.tufts.edu/hopper/text?doc=plat.+apol.+38a

Roy, Arundhati. "Is There Life After Democracy?". *Dawn. com*, May 7, 2009. http://www.dawn.com/news/475778/ is-there-life-after-democracy

Seibt, Johanna. "Process Philosophy", *The Stanford Encyclopedia of Philosophy* (Winter 2012 Edition). Ed. Edward N. Zalta, http://plato.stanford.edu/entries/process-philosophy/

Shaviro, Steve, ed. *Cognition and Decision in Non-Human Biological Organisms*. Living Books About Life series. Ann Arbor: Open Humanities Press, 2012. http://www. livingbooksaboutlife.org/books/Cognition_and_Decision

Shubin, Neil. *The Universe Within: A Scientific Adventure*. London: Allen Lane, 2013.

Stiegler, Bernard. *Technics and Time, 1: The Fault of Epimetheus*. Trans. Richard Beardsworth and George Collins. Stanford: Stanford University Press, 1998.

Swirski, Peter. "Lem in a Nutshell (Written Interview with Stanislaw Lem, July 1994)". *A Stanislaw Lem Reader*. Ed. Peter Swirski. Evanston: Northwestern University Press, 1997.

The Editors. "Why Efforts to Bring Extinct Species Back from the Dead Miss the Point". *Scientific American*, May 27, 2013. http://www.scientificamerican.com/article.cfm?id=why-efforts-bring-extinct-species-back-from-dead-miss-point

Zalasiewicz, Jan. *The Earth After Us: The Legacy That Humans Will Leave In The Rocks*. Oxford: Oxford University Press, 2008.

Zalasiewicz, Jan, Paul Crutzen and Will Steffen. "Anthropocene". *A Geologic Time Scale*. Ed. F. M. Gradstein *et al*. Cambridge: Cambridge University Press, 2012.

Zylinska, Joanna. *Bioethics in the Age of New Media*. Cambridge, MA: The MIT Press, 2009.

Zylinska, Joanna. "Bioethics Otherwise, or, How to Live with Machines, Humans, and Other Animals". *Telemorphosis: Theory in the Era of Climate Change*, Vol. 1. Ed. Tom Cohen. Ann Arbor: Open Humanities Press, 2012.

Zylinska, Joanna. "Evolution May Be Greater Than the Sum of Its Parts, But It's Not All That Great: On Lem's *Summa Technologiae*". Stanisław Lem, *Summa Technologiae*. Trans. Joanna Zylinska. Minneapolis: University of Minnesota Press, 2013.

88921374R00085

Made in the USA
Columbia, SC
14 February 2018